TEXAS
WIT

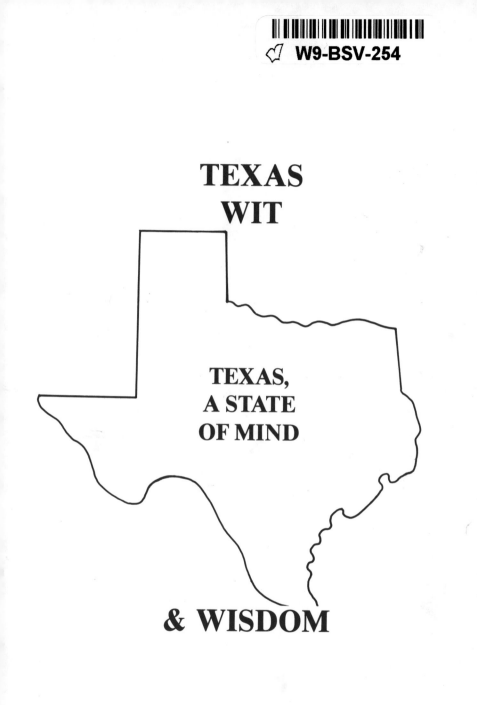

TEXAS,
A STATE
OF MIND

& WISDOM

TEXAS
WIT
& WISDOM

Wallace O. Chariton

Wordware Publishing, Inc.
REGIONAL DIVISION

Library of Congress Cataloging-in-Publication Data
Chariton, Wallace O.
  Texas wit and wisdom.

    1. Texas — Humor.   2. American wit and humor — Texas.
I. Title.
F386.6.C48   1989   976.4'00207   89-24942
ISBN 1-55622-257-2

ISBN 1-55622-257-2
10 9 8 7
8910

All inquiries for volume purchases of this book should be addressed to Wordware
Publishing, Inc. at the above address. Telephone inquiries may be made by calling:

(214) 423-0090

Contents

> *Never ask a man where he's from. If he's from Texas he'll tell you; if he isn't, you don't want to embarrass him.*

> *If you're messin' with Texas, you're messin' with a friend of mine.*

> *Only fools and newcomers predict Texas weather.*

> *Mary had a little lamb, what'll you have?*

> *Texas oil, good to the last drop.*

> *Many Texas towns are too small to support one lawyer, but none are too small to support two lawyers.*

> *Texas politics is proof you can fool all the people most of the time.*

Dedication

This book is dedicated to my good friend Glenn Raines, Jr., who is perhaps — just perhaps — the most honest used car salesman in Texas. That may explain why he always claims to be starving to death in the land of plenty.

If you should ever decide to trade cars with Glenn, my advice is do it quick. I know a man who swears he once haggled with Glenn for half an hour trying to get a lower price. Glenn finally gave in and said, "All right, I'll lower my price $200." But then he added, "Of course while we've been standing here arguing your trade-in has depreciated $300."

Acknowledgements

Since this book is a collection of Texas wit and wisdom, there are a lot of people who contributed either directly or indirectly. I would especially like to thank the following people who played a part whether they knew it or not.

First, I'd like to acknowledge the inadvertent help of such famous people as Lyndon Johnson, John Nance Garner, Darrell Royal, Sam Houston, William B. Travis, Sam Rayburn, Billie Sol Estes, Hondo Crouch, Joe Barton, Gib Lewis, Dick Yawes, Tom Landry, John Wayne, John Randolph, Blaine Nye, Tommy Nobis, Judge Roy Bean, Jerry Jones, Jimmy Johnson, Randy Galloway, Dutch Meter, Texas E. Schramm, Clint Murchison, H. L. Hunt, Sid Richardson, Glen McCarthy, Walt Garrison, Don Meredith, Bobby Layne, Ma and Pa Ferguson, W. Lee "Pappy" O'Daniel, Jerry Jeff Walker, Joe Don Looney, Bouce House, J. Frank Dobie, Walter Prescot Webb, Jerry Glanville, former Governer Pat Neff, present Governor Bill Clements, and possible future Governor Ann Richards.

I am indebted to Big Ed Wilks of Lubbock, Hal Jay, Joe Holsted, and Robert Shiflet of WBAP radio in Fort Worth, Paul Pryor of KLBJ radio in Austin, and John Downey of KILT radio in Houston. I also owe a large debt to Kevin McCarthy of KILF radio in Dallas. He was kind enough to allow me to request the help of his listeners to finish this book. Also thanks to KLIF listeners Dave Brownfield, Sarah Williamson, Lee Daken, and Tom Tomlinson. And a big thanks to Connie Herrera for helping me get on the program in the first place.

I'd be remiss if I didn't say thanks to Kirk Dooley, author of several outstanding books. Kirk allowed me to quote an Aggie joke from his *The Best of Texas.* Also thanks to Billy Porterfield of the *Austin American Statesman.* He gave me a wonderful quote from his review of my book *This Dog'll Hunt* and I appreciate it. I sincerely hope some of the other projects Billy and I have discussed come to pass.

Thanks to Glenn Raines of Dallas Motors. Not only did he help a starving author get some transportation but he contributed much to this book. And he always made me laugh when the days were darkest.

I would also like to say thanks to the Gigem Press for kindly allowing me to reprint some illustrations and other Aggie material.

Other contributors included Dennis Howard, who always seemed to have a new joke for me to consider, Lloyd Ash and Gayle Briscoe who tried to keep me up to date on various kinds of Texas material, Judy, Jennifer, and Gage Chariton for contributing just by being themselves.

I would also acknowledge the wonderful assistance of the staff of Wordware Publishing, Inc. with special recognition to Jana Gardner-Koch. In fact, the Aggie revenge chapter is especially dedicated to Jana. She knows why.

And finally, thanks to anyone whose name I might have omitted. So many people actually contributed to this effort that it is possible I failed to mention someone. If that happened, please write your name in the space provided. Then if we ever meet, and I hope we do, I'll be happy to sign the book as authentication that you did help.

Other contributors

An Introductory Letter to Virginia . . .

The Rumors of Our
Death Have Been
Greatly Exaggerated

Yes, Virginia, there is a Texas!

In the early 1950s the New York *Sun* published its reply to a young lady named Virginia who had written in asking if there really was a Santa Claus. Ed Creagh, who was writing for the Associated Press at the time, published his own version when he answered the mythical question from Virginia, "Is there any such place as Texas?"

Creagh replied, "No, Virginia, there isn't any Texas. Texas is just one of those good-natured myths — like Paul Bunyan, George Washington's cherry tree, or Brooklyn — that has been handed down, generation after generation, until many people have come to believe that it is true. It would be nice, wouldn't it, if there really was a Texas . . . But you're getting to be a big girl now, Virginia, and the truth must not be kept from you . . . Figure it out for yourself, Virginia: There couldn't be a Texas. No nation on earth, not even this rich and powerful land of ours, could afford a Texas. If Texas really existed, there wouldn't be room for the rest of us. Before you knew it, the whole country would be overrun by Texans. And that way lies madness."

This little Virginia is now, what, 45 or maybe 50 years old and it's time she learned the truth. So, in lieu of a formal introduction, I'd like to offer an open letter of rebuttal to that misguided little Yankee girl:

Dear Virginia,

Well, we haven't heard from you in a long time but I hope things have gone well with you. If you lead any sort of normal life, if such is possible in New York, then you probably grew up, got married, and had children of your own. If that's true, Virginia, then you are probably soon to be a grandmother, which is the reason I'm writing. It's one thing for you to be mislead about the existence of Texas, but it is another matter for you to not be able to tell your grandchildren the truth. So Virginia, get hold of yourself because there damn sure is a Texas!

Now Virginia, over the years you may have heard plenty about what you thought was a mythical state called Texas. A lot of what you heard was probably pure horse feathers, which is Texan for nonsense. Don't you believe it. A lot of people in other states are jealous of Texas and thus tend to make fun of the Lone Star State. Just listen to me, I'll set you straight.

It recent years, Texas has fallen on hard times, thanks to a bunch of camel jockeys messin' around with the price of oil. We hear down in Texas that many folks up north seem to believe we are about to dry up and blow away. Don't you believe that either. The rumors of our death have been greatly exaggerated. Texas has been through some tough times and there may be more ahead, but she will come back better than ever, if that's possible. You can count on it.

You should know, Virginia, that Texas is a very special place. It is the most unique state in America and the only state that was an independent, self-governed Republic before she chose to annex the United States. It is the largest state in the union (in terms of privately held, non-government land) and, according to many Texans, so much of what goes on in the Lone Star State is just naturally bigger or better than anywhere else in the world.

It's a shame that you couldn't grow up in Texas because the little girls in Texas just seem to turn out prettier than anywhere else, on the average. Since you couldn't grow up in Texas, I wish you could have married a Texan, assuming you married at all, because you would have probably gotten a nice tall man that could fight, drink, cuss, ride, and love with the best of 'em. And, if you'd been lucky and minded your manners, you just might have landed a husband with more money than God. Think about that the next time you bounce a check at the A&P.

I don't want to give you the impression that all Texans have a lot of money because they don't. And a lot of Texans that once had money are now so broke the banks won't let 'em draw breath. But Virginia, all Texans are rich in other ways. Texans live in the home of the brave and the land of the free; a place where the sunsets are out of this world and the moon is bigger, brighter, and more romantic than anywhere else on earth. We have the Alamo and San Jacinto, the beautiful hill country, the Spanish missions, the Big Bend National Park, the piney woods, plus some of the best hunting, fishing, football, and just fun in general to be found anywhere in the world. We have exotic foods, both kinds of music (country and western), plenty of wide open spaces, and more festivals than you could shake a stick at.

Texas has about anything you might want, from tall trees in East Texas to wide open plains in West Texas, to lush valleys along the Rio Grande in South Texas, to fancy metropolitan areas of North and Southeast Texas. In fact, about the only thing Texas doesn't have is a lot of snow. If you're a skier, that could be a problem because it is generally believed that if God had intended Texans to snow ski, he would have made manure white. On the other hand, the next time you or your husband spend half a day shoveling snow off your driveway, think about Texas. Also, while we don't snow ski, we do water ski, since Texas has more lakes than Minnesota, which bills itself as the land of a thousand lakes.

Now Virginia, I don't want you to start thinking Texas is a land of all milk and honey because that's not true. We do have serious problems, namely the weather and Yankees moving in. As for the weather, it does get a mite hot and humid on occasion. But for goodness sake, everything is air conditioned so the heat shouldn't bother you unless you're stupid enough to get out in it. In the winter, for those parts of Texas that actually have a winter, it does, on rare occasions, get somewhat cold. But we Texans have discovered fire, electricity, down jackets, long handle underwear, and furnaces so there's hardly ever any cases of entire families freezing to death.

The wind is, however, a different matter. In some parts of Texas the wind blows quite a bit, often kicking up a lot of dust. Why once out in Lubbock the dust was blowing so hard I actually saw a rabbit digging a hole and he was six feet off the ground at the time. And we do have an occasional tornado but I would venture the guess that more people have been killed by muggers in New York City than have been killed by Texas tornados. And tornados don't always kill. One of those twisters went through my living room several years back and I'm still alive. But I'll tell you this, Virginia, I'm a lot more religious now than I was before the tornado struck. It's just possible that God sends an occasional tornado into Texas to help keep the churches full. Some people have even suggested that God creates some bizarre Texas weather just to sort of balance out all the good things. If Texas always had great weather to go along with everything else that's great about the state, well hell's bells, Virginia, everyone on earth would want to live in Texas. And we just can't have that.

Of course, a lot of people already do want to live in Texas and a great many of 'em are Yankees. Why we've had so many Yankees moving in over the last couple of decades that in some places in Texas the hardest thing to find is a native Texan. While some resent this Yankee invasion, most Texans are not opposed to it because, after all, the state motto is friendship and what better way to be friendly than to welcome newcomers. But Virginia, what all Texans object to are the Yankees who come on down to Texas and then try to change the place and get us to do things their way. Apparently those yahoo Yankees forget that the reason they came to Texas in the first place was to get away from the way things are up north. So please, Virginia, if you ever have any friends who are thinking about relocating to Texas, tell them we don't give a damn how they did things up north. Will you do that for me, Virginia. I'd sure be much obliged.

I could go on and on about Texas, Virginia, but the best way for you to learn would be to come on down for a visit and see for yourself. Don't cut yourself short in the time department because there is a lot to see and do in Texas. You can enjoy everything from armadillo races to chili cook-offs to rattlesnake round-ups and about anything else you might like. If you've got 'em, bring the kids. They'd have fun at Six Flags, Astroworld, and Sea World. Plus they might see some real-life, sure 'nuff cowboys instead of those Rexall Rangers you have up in New York. And the little ones could ride some horses and see what a cow looks like before it ends up in the grocery store freezer. And if you want to find out if your husband has any romance left in him, just take him for a moonlight stroll along the San Antonio river walk. If that doesn't light a fire in his furnace, you might should start looking for a lawyer.

I would offer some advice before you come. First, being from New York, you probably talk funny with a strange accent. You may have some trouble making yourself understood, so plan to talk slow. You should also plan to listen slow. You see most Texans are proud of their state almost to a fault. A lot of what you'll hear is, well, call it overzealous exaggeration. Some people claim Texans have absolutely no regard for the truth, but that just isn't so. Quite the opposite in fact. Texans have such a high regard for the truth that they use it sparingly so as to not use it up. Of course, once you see Texas, you'll understand why we natives just sort of naturally brag about the place.

Another piece of advice I would offer is that when you come across the Red River, throw away any frowns you might have and put on a smile. You will find Texans a fun-loving, easy-living bunch that have little patience for sullen, cranky ol' Yankees who never smile and always complain. We Texans like to laugh and have a good time and you'll have more fun if you join right in. To get you started on Texas wit, I've attached a collection of some Texas humor that you might enjoy. Remember, Texans enjoy hearing and telling Texas jokes almost as much as they enjoy Yankee jokes. You should also know that Texans are not always funny and humorous. On occasion, some really profound thoughts and ideas have sprung from the minds of Texans. I have included a generous helping of Texas wisdom that will enlighten you and prove Texans have more in them than just hot air.

Well Virginia, I hope we have cleared the air and that you understand there really is a Texas. I also hope that you pay us a visit soon so you can see for yourself just how great this state really is. If you should have any questions about Texas, drop me a line and I'll try to help. Hope to see you soon.

Sincerely,
Wallace O. Chariton

P. S. If you should decide to come to Texas, please remember not to litter. After all, you'll be coming to God's country so don't mess with it. Thanks.

1

Texas and Texans

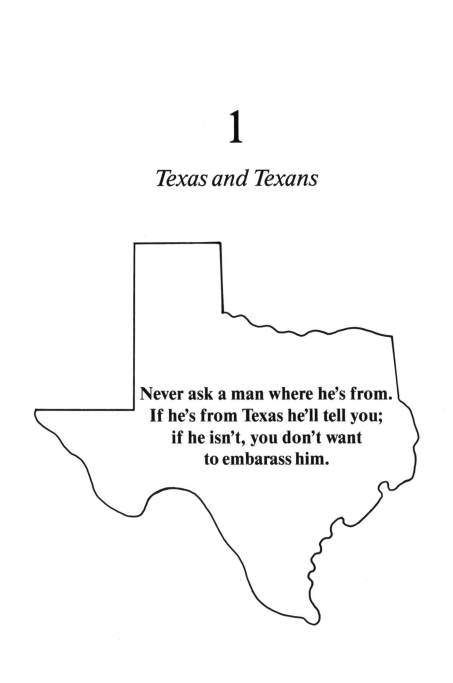

Never ask a man where he's from.
If he's from Texas he'll tell you;
if he isn't, you don't want
to embarass him.

For as long as there has been a Texas, there have been Texas jokes. Probably always will be. Everything about Texas — the good, the bad, the big, the pretty, and the ugly — is fair game for the jokesters. And you will generally hear the best Texas jokes from a Texan because, through it all, Texans seem to have a firm grip on their sense of humor. When the oil industry was booming, the oilmen usually told the best oil jokes. Now that the oil industry has gone bust, those same Texas oilmen are telling oil bust jokes even though they are the brunt of their own humor. And it is not at all unusual to hear the very best (and latest) Aggie jokes from Texas A&M students and graduates. And any Texan anywhere will tell you a joke about the weather.

One thing a lot of people seem to overlook about Texas is that in addition to humor, there have also been some intelligent things come out of the mouths and off the paper of Texans. The people who think Texans are country bumpkins ought to think again.

Even when you consider the size, the natural wonders, and the wealth of the state, the most unique thing about Texas is the people — the Texans. They have always had a high regard for their state and for the principals upon which the Republic of Texas was founded, most notably freedom from tyranny. A lot of Texans died trying to win freedom for their adopted land and a lot of them died trying to keep America free. The willingness to defend the cause of freedom created a fighting tradition which the famous J. Frank Dobie once said was a source of pride for the majority of Texans. The fact is, not all Texans are rich, or tall, or pretty, or handsome, or even smart. But many can fight, especially when they believe in the cause. As Robert E. Lee said during the Civil War: You never see the backs of Texans.

Of course, not all Texans go looking for fights. Some are lovers, some are wild bull riders, some are beauty queens, some are doctors, a lot are lawyers, and the vast majority are just plain ol' folks. But no matter the circumstances of the individual, they are Texans. Since this book is a collection of the wit and wisdom of the state of Texas, let's get started with a general sampling of both before we get too specific.

Roll on, Texas World famous humorist Will Rogers, who by all rights should have been a Texan, once observed, "Texas is a great state. It's the 'Old Man River' of states. No matter who runs it or what happens to it politically, it just keeps rolling along."

What is Texas? According to world-famous poet Carl Sandburg, "Texas is a blend of valor and swagger."

Happy Landing The man was perched on the ledge of a top floor window in a fifty-story downtown Dallas office building threatening to jump and end his life. The policeman was trying to prevent a tragedy. "Man," said the policeman, "don't jump. Think about your poor mother."

"She's passed on already."

"Ok, then remember your children," pleaded the policeman.

"Ain't got no children," the man replied.

"Well then," persisted the policeman, "remember your wife."

"Ain't got no wife either."

"Well for goodness sakes, remember the Alamo."

The man hesitated. "Alamo," he said, "what's that?"

The policeman didn't hesitate, "Go ahead and jump, you damn Yankee."

Words to Remember Robert Ruark once said, "Texan is what you are, not what you were or might be."

One reason Texans come from such strong stock is that when colonization of Texas was underway in the early 1800s, it was a rough trip. According to legend, only the bravest and strongest people made it to Texas. As for the others, the cowards never started the trip in the first place and the weak never finished it.

Medical History A poor old Texan was finally forced to go see a psychiatrist. His inferiority complex was bigger and better than anyone else.

The old philosopher Az Tex points out that before white men discovered Texas, the Indians were in charge. There were no traffic jams, taxes, very little crime, and women did all the work.

A Day That Will Live in Infamy Without question, the darkest day in the history of Texas was January 3, 1959. If you have to ask why, you might want to think real hard before calling yourself a Texan. If you absolutely have to look, the answer is on the last page.

Texas **B**umper **S**ticker Hall of Fame

Over the years, Texas creativity and wit has often shown through on stickers for car bumpers. Here is a sampling. Other members of the BS Hall of Fame will be found elsewhere.

♥ NY? Take INTERSTATE 30 East

The Texas answer to those "I Love NY" bumper stickers.

**We don't give a damn
how you did it up North!**

The Texas answer to Yankees who come down to Texas and try to get Texans to do things the way they're done up north.

**I'll never forgive mother for not having
the sense to be in Texas when I was born**

Texas Love it or leave it!

It's hard to be humble when you're from Texas

You can always tell a Texan, but you can't tell him much!

Drive Friendly
the life you save might be a Texan

Drive Friendly has long been a motto of the Texas Department of Public Safety. Some enterprising Texan added his own thoughts.

OK! I'm not a native Texan But I got here as soon as I could!

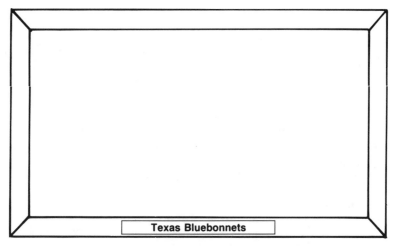

Texas Bluebonnets

Back during the 1940s John Randolph first published his clever little booklet Texas Brags. In the first and succeeding issues, Mr. Randolph always included a blank picture frame which he said was because the artist had yet to be born that could capture the beauty of the Texas state flower on canvas. That tradition is continued here since the artist still hasn't been born.

A True Texan   In *The Flavor of Texas,* J. Frank Dobie told a story relayed to him by Asa Jones which typifies the old-time perception of a real Texan. It seems Asa went over to New Orleans to do a little horse trading. One night he was awakened by the proprietor of the hotel, a widow woman, who was most concerned about a drunk who was causing quite a commotion in his attempt to get a room for the night. "I'll not have drunks in my hotel," she said.

The woman went on to say she had noticed from the guest register that Asa was from Texas and, such being the case, wondered if he wouldn't mind handling the ruffian. Apparently she assumed that anyone from Texas ought to be able to handle a Louisiana troublemaker. Naturally such a request caused some swelling in Asa's Texas pride. He went downstairs and disposed of the intruder in short order. "It was simply up to me to prove," he later told Dobie, "that I was a true Texian."

A Texas Classic   There was a highway patrolman once who was good about enforcing the law but a little slow in the spelling department. You can imagine his dismay when he was assigned to Waxahachie. At first not being able to spell the name of the town was a handicap until he had a brilliant idea. Everytime he needed to file a report, he simply drove twelve miles up the road and filed from Ennis. The trooper used that procedure for over two years and it always worked.

Then one day he received word that he was being sent to the FBI school in Washington for some advanced training in firearms. After two days of intense training the trooper decided to call one of his friends back in Texas and say hello. Unfortunately, he didn't know the number. He got the operator on the phone and said he wanted to speak to Billy Fred Bowie in Waxahachie, Texas. When the operator asked how to spell the name of the town, the trooper was embarrassed. "Hell, lady," he said, "if I knew how to spell it I'd a sent a post card and saved the cost of a phone call."

The operator finally figured it out and made the connection. But the trooper was so embarrassed he resolved to learn how to spell Waxahachie no matter how long it took. Sure enough, after he got home, he worked for over a month and finally learned the correct spelling. He was so happy he sent the following telegram to his boss down in Austin: Will no longer be filing reports from Ennis.

A couple of hours later his boss called to congratulate him and to let the poor trooper know he'd been transferred to Nacogdoches.

There is an old Texas saying: If God had intended Texans to ski, he'd a made manure white. Another version is: If God had intended people in Colorado to ski, he would have given them money.

Well, Have You? Goode Company Barbeque in Houston sells some of the best pecan pies in the entire state. The deluxe model comes in its own wooden shipping box. Burned into the lid of the box is a pointed question: Have you given any serious thought to thanking your lucky stars you're in Texas.

So You Wanna be a Texan! In a 1952 article for the *Dallas Morning News,* J. Frank Dobie said, "Texans are the only 'race of people' known to anthropologists who do not depend on breeding for propagation. Like princes and lords, they can be made by 'breath', plus a big hat — which comparatively few Texans wear."

More members of the Texas Bumper Sticker Hall of Fame. (Each one is on the Texas flag theme.)

A True Story? Boyce House, one of the greatest Texas humorists of all time, swore this was a true story. He was riding the train over in West Texas and struck up a conversation with a grizzled old rancher. When the train stopped for water, House and the rancher got off to stretch their legs. When they returned they found a rather rude gentlemen sprawled across both their seats reading a newspaper. The rancher politely explained that the stranger was in their seats and asked him to move. The stranger defiantly kept reading his newspaper and didn't even bother to reply. After a moment's wait, the rancher produced a Colt 45 from inside his jacket and whacked the stranger over the head.

"You've got five seconds to get out of those seats," demanded the rancher.

As the stranger hurried away rubbing his head, the rancher remarked, "It's fellas like that what give Texas a bad name."

A Texas Classic The oil company inspector, a native of Boston, was down in Midland looking over a new pipeline. Naturally, since the foreman on the job was a Texan, the conversation got around to the state heroes. The Texan went on and on about the men of the Alamo, Sam Houston, San Jacinto, the Texas Rangers, and even Audie Murphy.

When the foreman finally took a bragging break, the inspector commented, "We have heroes up north also."

"Oh yeah, like who?" asked the Texan.

"Well Paul Revere for one."

"Yeah," said the Texan, "Paul Revere, I've heard of him. Ain't he that fella that had to ride for help?"

Good Answer Have you heard about the old-timer who was once asked, "If you weren't a Texan, what would you be?"

His simple answer was "Ashamed."

Origin of Texas Someone once wrote: "Other states were carved or born; Texas grew from hide and horn." That may explain the famous quote by Noah Smithwick, an early Texas pioneer. He said, "Texas was heaven for men and dogs, but a hell for women and oxen."

He Got That Right Following the Civil War, Union General David Stanley made the following report to the Reconstruction Congress: "Texas is worse than any other state because she has never been whipped."

And Oil Hadn't Even Been Discovered During the early days of immigration to Texas, *The Guardian,* in Manchester England, reported to its readers: In Texas, no capital is needed except the sweat of a man's brow. Labor alone can make a man rich.

Postscript Maybe the editors of that publication based their observation on a famous quote by none other than Davy Crockett. On January 9, 1836, the "King of the Wild Frontier" wrote: "I must say as to what I have seen of Texas, it is the garden spot of the world. The best land and the best prospects for health I ever saw, and I do believe it is a fortune to any man to come here."

Travis the Prophet? In 1835 William B. Travis predicted, "Money must be raised or Texas is going to ruin." Funny how that still seems to be true today.

Congressman Joe Barton has a hat in his office that proclaims: American by choice, Texan by the grace of God.

From the Texas Bumper Sticker Hall of Fame even though this sticker was seen on a car in California.

Another Travis Prophecy "I think that Texas is forever ruined," wrote William B. Travis in 1835, "unless the citizens make a manly energetic effort to save themselves from anarchy and confusion, which are the worst of all evils. Let us march like a band of brothers."

From the Texas T-Shirt Hall of Fame.

How's That Again? Moses Austin, an early Texas pioneer, once commented, "I am already tired of the United States. It requires too much smartness, formality, politeness, dress, etc. to be considered respectable folks to suit someone who has lived in Texas as long as I have."

Texas a Religion? Stephen F. Austin said it: "The propriety of Texas has been the object of my labors — the idol of my existence — it has assumed the character of a religion — for the guidance of my thoughts and actions."

Be ALERT!
Texas needs more lerts

From the Texas Bumper Sticker Hall of Fame.

As strange as it seems, apparently some people actually don't like Texas. The following bumper sticker was recently seen in Richardson, Texas on a car with, you guessed it, New York plates: Yankee By Birth, Texan By Force.

Where Are You From? According to J. Frank Dobie: "A man from Iowa or Illinois will say 'I'm from the Middle West' . . . a Georgian or a Mississippian may admit to being merely a Southerner . . . but no Texan, given the opportunity, ever said otherwise than 'I'm from Texas.' "

Dobie Confirmation When Texas Senator William Blakley was asked if Texas was southern or western, he replied, "Texas is Texas."

Leave our Rock Alone! J. Frank Dobie, one of the great Texas writers, once wrote: "If I had to divide the population into classes today, I should characterize a goodly number as Texians, a very large number as Texans, and finally, all too many as just people who live in Texas. The Texians are the old rock itself; the Texans are out of the old rock; the others are wearing the rock away."

The problem is, Mr. Dobie put those words down on paper in 1936. That means more than fifty years of "rock erosion" has followed. If it doesn't stop soon, the "rock of Texas" will be nothing more than a kid's skipping stone.

The Right Blend   J. Frank Dobie once said that the pace of life in Texas "has the leisureliness of the old South, the manana-ness of Mexico, and the waiting quality of the Indian."

101% TEXAN!

From the Texas Bumper Sticker Hall of Fame. This saying is also popular on T-Shirts, caps, and hat pins.

My Thoughts Exactly   In her wonderful book *I'll Take Texas,* Mary Lasswell commented, "I am forced to conclude that God made Texas on his day off, for pure entertainment, just to prove what diversity could be crammed into one section of earth by a really top hand."

Another Accurate Description   Here is Walter Prescot Webb's famous description of the Big Bend area of Texas: "There it lies in its gorgeous splendor and geological confusion, almost as if it fell from the hands of its Creator. It fascinates every observer because it seems to be made of the scraps left over when the world was made, containing samples of rivers, deserts, blocks of sunken mountains, and tree-clad peaks, dried-up lakes, canyons, cuestas, vegas, playas, arroyos, volcanic refuse, and hot springs."

Fact or Fiction?   One of the most famous residents of North Dallas is Charlie Pride, the great country-western singer. When Charlie moved in, he was not only the first famous singer in the area, he was also one of the first blacks. In case you don't know, there was a time when black families in North Dallas were about as rare as wisdom teeth in a rooster. Naturally the arrival of the Pride family gave birth to several legends.

The most famous story had Charlie out mowing his lawn one day when a neighbor lady, who was unaccustomed to seeing blacks in the area, happened by and assumed he was the yard man. She stopped and inquired how much he would charge to mow her lawn. For Fun, Charlie quoted her a price and she agreed. To continue the joke, Charlie actually mowed the lady's lawn but when it came time to collect, he threw the neighbor a curve. One of Charlie's best friends happened to be in town and Charlie asked him to go collect the bill. The friend agreed and you can imagine the neighbor's surprise when Elvis Presley showed up at her door asking for the cash.

In another instance, Charlie's daughter was having trouble making friends, so when a neighbor girl invited the little Miss Pride to her birthday, naturally Charlie was happy. So happy in fact, that he and Elvis showed up at the party to entertain the youngsters. Undoubtedly it would have have been the most famous birthday party in Texas if the story were true. No such luck. On a recent radio talk show, I asked Charlie about the stories. He laughed and said that over the years he had heard many versions of the stories and, sadly, not a single one is true.

LBJ Wisdom Lyndon Johnson once commented, "A long time ago down in Texas I learned that telling a man to go to hell and making him go there are two different propositions."

Texas Riddle No. 1: What has a mouth but never speaks and a bed but never sleeps? See answers on the last page.

He Has a Great Mother Jose Antonio Navarro once wrote from Acordada Prison in Mexico: "I have sworn to be a good Texan, and that I will not forswear. I will die for that which I firmly believe, for I know it is just and right. One life is a small price for a cause so great. As I fought, so shall I be willing to die. I will never forsake Texas and her cause. I am her son."

May She Never Change John C. B. Richmond once said, "Texas is still a last frontier. It's the part of the United States where the traditional virtues are still operating. In short, a piece of living history."

But Not Much Bigger? Noted physicist Dr. Werner von Braun was once asked about the possibility of satellites colliding in space. He replied, "You must remember that space is large; it is even larger than Texas."

And So Many Yankees Have Saws In *The Searchers,* John Wayne had a classic line: "A Texan ain't nothing but a human being way out on a limb."

Ain't it the Truth Sam Houston once observed, "Texas could get along without the United States, but the United States cannot, except at great hazard, exist without Texas." It was also Houston who commented on the prospects of annexation, "We surrender everything and, in reality, we get nothing, only protection."

More Houston Wisdom In 1858 war clouds were gathering in the South and there was already talk in Texas about withdrawing from the Union and joining a new Southern Confederacy. Sam Houston, governor of

Texas at the time, felt joining the confederacy would be a mistake. He had a better idea, as detailed in this excerpt from one of his speeches: "If the principals are disregarded upon which the annexation of Texas was consummated — Louisiana was a purchase; California, New Mexico, and Utah, a conquest; but Texas was a voluntary annexation — sorrowing for the mistake she made in sacrificing her independence on the alter of her patriotism, she would unfurl again the banner of the Lone Star to the breeze and reenter upon a national career." If only more people had listened to Houston, this very day, New Mexico, Arizona, Southern California, and parts of Mexico might be states in the Republic of Texas. But no one listened.

No Doubt About It Sam Houston once said, "Texas is the finest portion of the globe that has ever blessed my vision."

WARNING! I brake for Giant Armadillos!

From the Texas Bumper Sticker Hall of Fame. Several years ago Lone Star Brewery out of San Antonio, Texas ran a very popular Giant Armadillo campaign. Naturally there were creative contributions by witty Texans. This was a popular bumper sticker, but the most innovative contribution was the man who sold giant armadillo insurance.

Longnecks and Cowboys No Place but Texas

Lone Star Beer also helped make the longneck beer bottle popular. To support their effort, numerous bumper stickers appeared with various sayings. Naturally, Texans quickly got on the "nowhere but" theme and published their own versions. At the University of Texas, a popular version was "Longhorns and Longnecks, No Place But Austin." Naturally, the Aggies countered with, "Steers and Queers, No Place But Austin."

Another Texas Description Someone once said: "Texas has more trees and less timber; more rivers and less water; more resources and less cash; more itinerant preachers and less religion; more cows and less milk, and you can see farther and see less than any damn country in the world."

A Texas Classic Two traveling salesmen were on the road making their rounds when they spotted a sign which read Mexia, 15 miles. Naturally the two men quickly got into an argument about how to pronounce the name of the small Texas town. "It's Mex-e-a," offered one. "No, it's Ma-hay-ya," countered the other. The friendly argument continued while they covered those 15 miles; so when they reached the town, they decided to stop and ask a local to solve the dilemma. The driver wheeled into the first business establishment he came to and both men marched inside to get the elusive answer.

As a young lady approached, one of the peddlers asked, "Miss, could you please settle an argument and tell us how to pronounce the name of this place?"

"Sure," she said, smiling broadly, "It's Dairy Queen."

Rest of the Story I was recently driving through Mexia and happened to pass the local Dairy Queen. I decided to test the old joke and marched inside. Unfortunately, to my dismay, the waitress had heard the joke many times. "But," she added, "it's wrong."

"Wrong?" I asked. "What do you mean?"

"The old-timers around here don't pronounce the name as Ma-hay-ya. It's Ma-hayer."

"It's what?" I asked.

She grabbed a lock of almost bright red hair and said, "It's Ma-hayer, you know, like My-hair."

Parental Direction There was a small Texan who was almost ten years old before his parents finally told him that "Damn Yankee" was actually two words. That same youngster was packing to go away for college when his parents finally broke down and told him about Alaska being admitted to the Union.

Go Ahead, Do It The state tourism bureau urges visitors to: Have a big time in Texas.

Friendship State The state motto of Texas is friendly. Even the motto you are encouraged to use on the roads is Drive Friendly. That old philosopher Az Tex suggests if you want to find out how many friends you have in Texas, just buy a weekend get-away condo on Padre Island.

Maps similar to the above have been published for generations as souvenir items of Texas. Many northern families have taken these exaggerated maps home not realizing they could do harm to their children. In one case, a youngster in Washington state had one of the maps and assumed it to be true. When his family announced they were driving to Chicago for vacation the boy was all excited. But when they arrived, he was disappointed. When his mother asked what the problem was, the youngster replied, "This can't be Chicago because we didn't go through Texas."

You're on the Air This is an absolutely true story. There is an old saying in Texas that the difference between a Yankee and a damn Yankee is that the Yankee has the sense to stay where he belongs. A television newsman in Houston once told a slightly different version on the air: "Yankees who come to Texas are a lot like hemorrhoids," he said. "Those that come down and go back up are no big problem; but those that come down and stay are trouble." Needless to stay, considering the high density of Northern transplants in the Bayou City, the station's switchboard lit up like a Christmas tree. As for the newsman? He hasn't been seen in a number of years.

Postscript A modern version of the Yankee problem is now circulating. According to the story, the Lone Star State has set some sort of record because, with all the Yankees moving in, Texas is now the only state in the Union with more horses' butts than horses.

In driving around Texas, it is possible to spot some wild and wooly critters. Small herds of buffalo or longhorn cattle can occasionally be seen in some rancher's fence. Out in Lubbock's MacKenzie park there's an entire town of almost extinct prairie dogs; and down on the YO Ranch in South Texas you can see some exotic animals that you would expect to see running wild in Africa or in a zoo. Several landowners have been known to keep big cats in various breeds ranging from leopards, to cougars, all the way to the king of beasts himself.

Perhaps the most exotic of all animals in Texas might be the hippopotamus owned by one hill country rancher. Not long ago Harriet the Hippo escaped from her fenced pasture and wandered off down Highway 16 toward Bandera looking for wild flowers to munch on. After causing more than a few motorists to do a double take, Harriet was finally corralled and loaded into a trailer for a ride back home. Although gentle as a lamb, loading Harriet was a problem because, as veterinarian Mark Richardson explained, "There's no handles on a hippopotamus."

A Texas Classic A traveling salesman arrived in El Paso from the west coast and sent a FAX to his home office in Kansas City. The general sales manager sent a FAX back for him to run over to Texarkana and collect a past due account. The salesman returned another FAX, "You run over there and collect it yourself, you're closer than I am."

Little Texans Contribute Little Meredith Marr was excited that her mother was expecting another child. Meredith was certain the new arrival would be a sister for her to play with but unfortunately the ultra sound indicated the new baby would be male. When told the news, Meredth was disappointed. She turned to a friend and exclaimed, "My baby sister is a boy."

A Mystery In a recent issue of the Fort Worth *Star Telegram*, the editors quoted an article that first appeared in the *Texas Gazette* in 1830. The article was actually a letter originally sent to the editors of the *Gazette* from a man who had moved from Kentucky to Texas, and he was explaining how much better things were in Texas. At one point the man said, according to the *Star Telegram*, "Hemp I dare say would grow better here [Texas] than in Kentucky, but I think, for cables or strong ropes, the *cabrista*, or rope made of the wild hore hair, preferable to those made of hemp." Obviously someone, either the *Star Telegram* or the original *Gazette*, left a letter out of the word "hore." The mystery is, what letter was omitted. Did they omit an 's' between the 'r' and 'e' or was the word supposed to begin with a 'w?' We'll probably never know, but if the word was supposed to start with a w, that might explain why good ropes were always in short supply in early Texas.

How Big is Texas? In the covered wagon days, if a baby was born in Texarkana while the family was crossing the Lone Star State, by the time they reached El Paso, the baby would be in the third grade.

Fertile Ground The land in some parts of Texas is so fertile it is said you could plant a tenpenny nail and grow a railroad spike. For ladies, they could plant a penny in their garden and grow a fine copper tea kettle.

Another Little Texan Contributes Jennifer Chariton was about three when we went to the Dairy Queen for some ice cream. I ordered a dip cone, which is vanilla ice cream dipped in chocolate. Jennifer asked for the same, not really knowing what it was. "No," I replied, "you can have a plain cone."

Jennifer immediately erupted into tears. "What's wrong," I asked.

"Daddy," she said through the tears, "I don't want a plain cone. I want one with ice cream in it."

There are two
kinds of people
TEXANS
and those who
wish they were

From the Texas T-Shirt Hall of Fame.

Still Another Young Texan Strikes The mom was having some of the ladies over for tea. She was busy entertaining so she asked her daughter to prepare the tea, which the little girl did promptly. Naturally, the guests went on and on about how good the tea was to make the little girl feel good. After about the tenth compliment, the daughter sighed heavily. "Oh, I'm so glad you like it," she said, "I was afraid it wouldn't be good."

"And why is that dear," mom asked.

"Well," replied the little girl, "I couldn't find the tea strainer so I used the fly swatter."

That old philosopher Az Tex swears he saw a gorgeous Texas beauty that was wearin' her jeans so tight that he could hardly breath.

19

A Texas Classic The Texan was visiting relatives up North and they took him to see Niagara Falls. "I bet you don't have anything like that in Texas," commented one of the relatives.

The Texan thought for a moment, then replied, "No sir, we don't. But we got a plumber in Fort Worth that could fix that leak in half an hour."

A Favorite Lyndon Johnson Story When the war between the states flared up, a young Texan enlisted and marched off to fight with his friends. "We won't be gone long," he claimed, "cause we can lick them Yankees with broom sticks."

Four years later when the fighting was finally over, the young man came home, a beaten man. One of his neighbors asked, "What happened? I thought you was gonna beat them Yankees with broom sticks?"

We could have, replied the young man, "Except we couldn't get 'em to fight with broomsticks."

Another Johnson Story A young Texan asked if he could go to town with his older brother. When told no, he replied, "It ain't fair. My brother has been twowheres and I ain't never been nowheres."

Ain't it the Truth Don Graham, author of *Cowboys and Cadillacs,* observed "Texans have two pasts: one made in Texas, one made in Hollywood."

It's Still True In 1844, Jane McManus Cazneau said, "Texas, the gathering place of the most restless and imaginative spirits in the union, inclines naturally to the romantic."

From the Texas T-Shirt Hall of Fame. Gage Chariton has a different version of the saying, which he claims to have invented. When asked where he's from, he replies, "I was born and bred below the Red."

Did you hear about the Texan who wanted to start collecting miniatures so he bought Rhode Island.

Very Great Indeed A New York newspaper reported in 1847 that, "Texas is a great country but they have some very great liars there."

Friendly Feuding Texas is actually so big that the state contains many diverse areas which naturally leads to some friendly feuding within the state. Here are some quick examples:

People in East Texas claim West Texas is so flat you can stand on one tuna fish can and see another one 100 miles away.

People in West Texas claim there isn't anything to see in East Texas because all the damn trees get in the way.

The people in East Texas believe that the fastest dogs in the world are located in West Texas. The dogs out west have to be fast because the trees are so far apart.

Texans in the hill country will tell any other part of the state that when hill country folks die there is no need for them to go to heaven because they are already there.

People in North Texas claim Houston is the world's largest sauna bath because of the humidity. Houstonians, on the other hand, stay away from Dallas because they don't want to be surrounded by Yankees.

Many years ago a Dallas writer claimed the pace of industry in Fort Worth was so slow that it was possible to see a panther napping on one of that city's busiest streets. Naturally, for years Fort Worth was known as "Panther City." Fort Worth citizens countered that Dallas was trying to be the "Manhattan of the West" which meant Dallas was where the East petered out and Fort Worth was where the West began.

Out in West Texas, there's a saying: Raise hell in Midland, raise your kids in Odessa. Or is that the other way around?

Air travel isn't always convenient in some parts of Texas. Out in Lubbock, for instances, they have a saying: If you die and go to hell, you'll have to go through Dallas. Funny how they never mention dying and going to heaven.

Of course, when Texans aren't poking fun at each other, Oklahoma is a frequent target. It has been speculated that the only reason God invented Oklahoma was so he would have something to put between Texas and Kansas. And then my friend Dwain Heath, that old Baylor Bear, swears that everytime he goes to Oklahoma he turns the clock back twenty years.

Texas Tale Spinning

Texans — real, authentic, Texans — have a natural tendency to tell tales about their state. Lon Tinkle, a much respected Texas writer, once observed, "Texans have ample reasons to be proud of their heritage, even to brag." It is generally accepted as fact that most any Texan can be depended on to make a short story long which comes natural because old Texans don't die, they just get a new tale. But what most people don't realize is that tale spinning (or bragging) is actually an art that usually takes years to perfect. And there are strict rules that must be followed.

The first rule in the art of telling a tale is that you must talk about something you know. For instance, you would never have a norther strike in July because they just don't do that. You would never tell a fishing whopper about a kind of fish that isn't caught in Texas.

The second rule for spinning a tale is that your story should be just on the fringes of believability — not too absurd that you are dismissed immediately as a braggart.

The third rule is simply that you *must* deliver the tale with utmost sincerity. Tell the story like you actually believe it, with lots of emphasis for effect.

The fourth rule is that whenever possible, you ought to have a bit of surprise in your ending. As an example:

My uncle once sent me into town in the pickup to order a load of gasoline to be used in the farm equipment. When I got there, the man said his tank truck was broke down and it'd be a week before the gas could be delivered. Well I knew that wouldn't do since my uncle needed fuel right away. To resolve the problem, I put several open 55-gallon drums in the back of the truck, filled 'em up with high octane, and headed home driving carefully so the gas wouldn't slosh out. On the way I decided to sneak a smoke and, sure enough, I forgot what I was carrying and tossed the burning match out the window. Naturally, it landed in one of those open 55-gallon drums of gasoline.

Now, what ending would you expect? Something like, the truck blew up and beat me home? No, that's not it. What actually happened was, when I realized what I had done I jumped out of the truck and I was lucky enough to only lose a gallon and a half of gasoline before I got the fire out.

The final rule for Texas tale spinning is that you never, ever, under any circumstances admit you weren't telling the truth. Here's a Texas tale that adheres nicely to all the rules:

I was out walking barefoot through a fresh plowed field, which is one of the pleasures in life everyone should experience. As I walked along squishing loose dirt between my toes, I heard a sudden commotion. I looked up to see a giant hawk, only slightly larger than an eagle, zeroing in on one of the largest Texas jackrabbits you ever say. In fact that rabbit was so big I first thought it was a young calf.

Well ol' Mr. Jackrabbit had no desire to be lunch for some dang ol' bird so he was running for all he was worth. The only problem was, the hawk was gaining on him. I have no doubt that hawk would a caught the rabbit if Mr. Jack hadn't run under a barbed wire fence and jerked to a halt. He just sat there, under the last strand of wire, and tried to catch his breath.

Well, of course, the hawk couldn't swoop down while the rabbit was under the fence for fear his wings would get caught in the wires. Naturally the rabbit noticed the hawk was keeping his distance and apparently he felt safe. So instead of continuing to run, the rabbit simply stayed under the fence, content to wait till the bird of prey moved on.

Now the rabbit's plan might have worked except that the hawk was also pretty smart. Instead of giving up, the hawk merely landed on a nearby fence post to wait until the rabbit came out. Clearly this was developing into a battle of nerves and I decided to watch to see how it turned out. I laid down under an old scrub oak tree and chewed on a blade of grass while I watched the action.

Mr. Jack was having a tough time, let me tell you. He knew he was trapped like a frog under a bucket and there wasn't nuthin' he could do so long as the hawk rested ominously on the fence post. The poor rabbit was so nervous he sort of paced the ground between posts, making sure he never strayed out from under the bottom wire. For the better part of an hour, me and that hawk watched as that rabbit paced back and worth wearin' down the ground.

I was still watchin' the show when I became aware of some hot air on one of my bare feet. When I turned around to look, I came face to face with 2,500 pounds of the meanest looking bull you would ever want to see. Obviously I had wandered into the bull's pasture by mistake and he wasn't any too happy about it. I quickly decided that I'd been too hard for my mother to raise to allow some bull to stick a horn in me, so I broke and ran for the fence. Since the place where that rabbit was trapped was the closet to me, I headed straight for it.

There I was flying across the pasture with my shirt tail flappin' and a mean bull following right behind. As I got near the fence, two things happened. First, the hawk, who must have wondered what in the hell was going on, took flight. Second, I realized the fence was too high, and time was too short, to allow for me to climb over. If I was to get away from the bull, my only chance was to dive under, which I promptly did when I got to the fence. Now I want to tell you I was a big ol' kid, and I sure couldn't have easily fit under that fence without getting some serious scratches and probably losing the seat out of my jeans. But that rabbit, bless his heart, had done so much pacing, that he moved just enough dirt to allow me to slide under.

Once under the fence, I was probably safe but I decided to run on home anyway. When I chanced a look back, that ol' bull was doing his best to tear down the fence, so I ran a little harder just in case he made it. I had gone about a hundred yards when I heard the hawk scream. I looked up and saw him circling overheard, obviously upset. When I looked down I saw why — that rabbit was running along right beside me, in second gear so he wouldn't outrun me. I tell you that rabbit was the smartest thing. He figured out that the hawk wouldn't attack while I was around, so the rabbit just loped along beside me for about two hundred yards until we came to a small stand of woods with thick underbrush. At that point, Mr. Jack veered off to the right and disappeared into the brush where he would be safe from man and hawk. When the rabbit got into the edge of the brush, he stopped and looked back at me. If I didn't know better, I'd swear he smiled at me.

Well, I ran all the way home to safety. I never saw that bull again but I heard he got killed a couple of weeks later when he tried to chase a freight train out of his pasture. As for the hawk, the last I heard he had built a nest in one of the tall tress in that stand of woods, apparently determined to get the rabbit no matter how long it took. And concerning Mr. Jack, as far as I know, he's probably still in that brush waiting for me to come back and get him out.

2

Don't Mess with Texas

If you're messin'
with Texas,
you're messin' with
a friend of mine.

Jerry Jeff Walker

One thing Texas has plenty of is highways. It is often said when you drive across Texas, you see miles and miles of nothing but miles and miles. When you have as many highway miles as Texas, litter is an inevitable problem. And the state of Texas is serious about litter because it costs so much to clean up after more than seventeen million people, which doesn't count the millions of visitors who come to Texas each year.

Over the years, Texas has tried many slogans to discourage littering. Two popular ones were:

Littering
is
unlAWFUL

and

Picking up YOUR litter
off YOUR highway
costs YOU money.

One small Texas town was so interested in cleaning up its act that there is a story circulating about the town having passed an ordinance whereby there is a $50 dollar fine for anyone caught telling dirty jokes. If that's true, watch out for the richest little town in the world.

Without doubt, the most popular slogan to come along in years is the now famous: Don't Mess With Texas. While I don't know who came up with the slogan, he (or she) is to be commended. Although some Texans (my mother included) don't like the slogan because they think it sounds a little braggadocios, I would say "and well it should." Texas needs to regain that old "Don't Mess with Us" spirit and if some litter signs help in the cause, let it rip.

For most, the saying has really caught on. You can find it on T-Shirts, bumper stickers, and caps just about anywhere in Texas. And of course, the slogan has found its way to the side of the Texas highways.

Signs like this are often seen at the entrances of roadside parks in Texas. Two things about the signs are worthy of some note. First, the phrase "save taxes" is appropriately shown inside the barrel, demonstrating that when you litter you are actually throwing away money. The second point of interest on this sign is the "No Soliciting" addition. One can't help but wonder if that might not be intended for the prostitutes that have known to frequent rest stops late at night looking for lonely truckers who have stopped for some rest.

The Don't Mess With Texas stickers show up almost anywhere.

The above bumper sticker is one given away by Congressman Joe Barton (6th District) in his Washington offices.

To drive home the point of not messing with Texas, the state has solicited the aid of some famous sports figures. In one commercial, Ed Jones and Randy White of the Dallas Cowboys are shown picking up what someone else left behind. The spot ends with Mr. White (I don't know about you but that's what I call him) giving the viewer the sincere impression he'd like to be left alone for just a few minutes with anyone caught littering. No thank you very much.

In another anti-litter commercial, Nolan Ryan, that fire-balling, big league pitcher out of Alvin, Texas, is shown wadding up a piece of litter and then firing it toward a litter barrel, which promptly explodes as if being hit by a mortar round. Another anti-litter campaign using the Don't mess with Texas theme comes via songs featuring noted Texas crooners. Adopted son and pretty fair country picker Jerry Jeff Walker sang to all telling everyone pointedly, "If you mess with Texas, you're messing with a friend of mine." But the king of Texas pickers and grinners, Willie Nelson, may have had the best line when he sang, "Mammas, just tell your babies, Don't mess with Texas." It's a shame he didn't add a line, "But if they do mess with Texas, make sure they're wearing Pampers."

Related Messing The Don't Mess With Texas slogan was intended to encourage people not to litter along the state's highways. But Texans, being an inventive bunch, have found other uses. Not long after the slogan was debuted, the Red Raiders of Texas Tech defeated the Longhorns of the University of Texas in football. Almost before the lights in Jones Stadium were turned off, someone was on the streets selling T-shirts proclaiming: "We messed with Texas." Although that actually happened several years ago, as late as June of 1989 at least one young lady in Lubbock was still wearing her T-shirt.

Down in Austin there's a Mexican restaurant selling T-shirts proclaiming: "Don't mess with Tex-Mex." Also out in Lubbock, Innergas has adopted a similar saying on a billboard: "Don't let 'em mess with your furnace." When Jackie Sherrill was still the head football coach at Texas A&M and his program came under fire, a popular bumper sticker in and around College Station, Texas was "Don't Mess with Jackie's Aggies."

Related Story A good friend who is opposed to any more Yankees coming down to Texas and staying wants to launch a "Don't Mesh with Texas" program.

Unfriendly Messin' Not all of the useage of the Don't Mess With Texas slogan is friendly. Out in Lubbock, Texas not long ago a terrorist group (terrorists in Lubbock?) broke into a laboratory on the Texas Tech campus. The group which calls itself the Animal Liberation Front, or ALF for short, vandalized the offices and stole some cats that were being used in critical sleep disorder experiments. The ALF marauders left behind a message painted on a wall, "Don't Mess with Texas Animals."

A popular Texas bumper sticker which indicates how many Texans feel about possible gun control.

I'm the only one that can mess with Texas.

From the Texas T-Shirt Hall of Fame. Perhaps the most creative use of the Don't Mess With Texas theme.

> If you value your life as much as I value this truck, you won't mess with it.

The Don't Mess With theme used to illustrate how some Texans feel about their pickup trucks.

That old philosopher Az Tex wonders how much money could be saved if everyone would stop littering so the state wouldn't have to spend so much money on signs.

And finally, concerning litter, a friend has sent his idea for some new signs. His version is:

Unless your mother is
following you to pick up
your litter, don't do it.

31

3

Texas Weather Watch

**Only fools and newcomers
predict Texas weather**

The one aspect of life in Texas that is probably the subject of the most humor is the weather. J. Frank Dobie once said, "One Texas claim is that it does not have a climate, just weather." It has often been said that if you don't like the weather in the Lone Star State, you can either wait a minute and it will change or you can step across the street and the weather will be different. But don't ever try to predict Texas weather; that honor is generally reserved for fools and newcomers.

Without doubt, the one aspect of Texas weather that gets the most attention is the famous northers. Generally a norther is a severe, rapid moving cold front that descends upon Texas from, you guessed it, the north. The Texas norther, according to the old ballad, "Comes sudden and soon; in the dead of night or the blaze of noon."

Northers have been known to drop temperatures as much as 50 degrees in just a couple of hours. They have been associated with howling, icy winds, large hail, and an occasional tornado. The most famous norther is the blue one, which pushes clouds ahead of it giving the appearance of a blue color on the horizon. A dry norther is one that simply produces cold temperatures without moisture. Either way, when a furious Texas norther strikes, you can be in for trouble if you aren't prepared. Naturally, because the northers are so dramatic, they have been the object of considerable Texas humor. Other than northers, the other five elements of Texas weather most often cussed and discussed are heat, cold, wet, dry, and windy, in no particular order of importance. Here's a vintage collection of weather humor.

How Dry Was It?   It was so dry the cows were giving evaporated milk.

A farmer was walking out to the barn one night to check his stock. A norther struck sudden like and froze the flame in the lantern. Without thinking, the farmer broke off the flame and pitched it aside. Sure enough, when the weather cleared up, the flame thawed, caught the grass on fire, and ended up burning down the man's barn.

How Hot Was It?   It was so hot, I saw a rattlesnake crawl into a camp fire looking for shade under the coffee pot.

How Cold Was It? It was so cold that a 32 degree Mason dropped two degrees.

The best ever wind story involved a New Yorker who came to Texas and purchased a section of land from a well known rancher. The day after they signed the papers, a famous West Texas dust storm struck and when it was over, that New Yorker's piece of ground had blown away. He searched for it several days without results. Finally he ran an ad in the lost and found section of the paper. He got several calls and inspected many sections of land but none of them were his. He finally gave up and went back to New York, and to this day that section of land has not turned up.

How Hot Was It? It was so hot the birds had to use pot holders to pull the worms out of their holes.

How Bad Was the Drought? Water was so scarce we not only had to plow under the cotton, but we had to plow under the hogs as well.

A Texas Classic The old farmer was out plowing behind his favorite two mules. The heat was sweltering and finally one of the mules up and died from sunstroke. The farmer unhooked the live mule and mounted up for a nice ride back to the barn. A sudden norther struck and the farmer rode for all the mule was worth and he barely managed to stay in front of the icy winds. As the farmer reached the barn, he discovered the front of the poor ol' mule was frothy with sweat while the hindquarters were frozen solid.

The farmer's clothes were also frozen so his wife stood him in front of the fire to warm up. Unfortunately, when his clothes thawed, the water flooded the room and put out the fire.

How Windy Was It? It was so windy I saw a chicken lay the same egg three times.

How Hot Was It? It was so hot the chickens were plucking themselves.

The old farmer was asked by a friend if he'd gotten any rain lately. "Sure have," he replied, "we got a three-inch rain just this morning."

"Really," the friend replied, "it sure seems dry to have gotten that much rain this morning."

"Well you must remember," the farmer added, "that out here a three-inch rain means there was three inches between drops."

How Dry Was It? It was so dry the service stations were giving away gasoline and charging $20 to fill up your radiator.

That old philosopher Az Tex advises: You know you've been through a tornado when your garage door stays down but your house goes up.

How Hot Was It? It was hot enough to melt the shoes off a horse.

A Texas Classic An old settler from back east had finally had enough of trying to make a go of it on the harsh Texas prairie. He loaded up all of his possessions, including his family, and headed for town. An acquaintance noticed that the settler's wagon was being pulled by a scrawny old mare horse teamed with a pitiful excuse for an ox and inquired as to what had happened to the man's other horse.

"The drought got so bad that my other horse just couldn't take it any longer and he up and died on me. So I traded for this here ox."

"What'd you trade?" asked the friend.

"Well," the settler replied, "I had those two sections of the poorest hardscrabble land on earth so I traded one of 'em for the ox."

The friend shook his head. "Sounds like a pretty steep trade to me."

"I'm satisfied," replied the settler. "When we sat down to make out the papers, I found out the damned old fool I was tradin' with couldn't read; so I made out the deed myself and stuck him with both sections."

How Dry Was It? It gets so dry that in some parts of West Texas the citizens have to fasten stamps on letter with safety pins.

Big Ed Wilks, long time radio man in Lubbock was recently asked if that part of Texas was getting any rain. "Yes," he replied, "we've had about 18 inches this year. But unfortunately, I missed every drop. I was out of town that day."

Rain is always a big story in Texas but on occasion it can cause problems for newsmen. Once when a much needed rain came along to end an extensive drought, it also caused a flood which took several lives. After some study on how to report the event, a newsman came up with the following headline: Beneficial rains cause 10 deaths in West Texas.

How Dry Was It? It is so dry out in West Texas that a man in Lubbock swears that after a rare downpour, he checked his rain gauge and found three inches of dust.

How Cold Was It? It was so cold the tobacco chewers were spitting brown ice cubes.

A Texas Classic Texas weather always seems to find its way into print. Once, during early fall in a small Texas town, the weather man predicted the season's first freeze for the following day. The reporter, knowing the first freeze was usually a signal to farmers to slaughter hogs in preparation for the long hard winter, began his story with, "Tomorrow will be hog killing weather." Unfortunately, the paper's headline writer was newly arrived from some city up north, so after reading the lead, he composed the following headline for the story: FARMERS, PROTECT YOUR HOGS.

A tourist asked a West Texas filling station attendant, "Does it ever rain around here?"

"It sure does," he replied. "Have you read in the Bible about when it rained for forty days and forty nights?"

"Of course," she replied, "I'm familiar with Noah's flood."

"Well," the farmer said proudly, "out here in West Texas we got nearly two and a half inches during that spell."

How Cold Was It? It was cold enough to freeze the balls off a billiard table.

Strange But True The Texas wind has been known to turn a prairie dog hole inside out, blow the feathers off chickens, and carry a dozen farmhouses away without disturbing the mortgages on the houses.

Amarillo is reputed to have nothing between the city and the North Pole except a barbed wire fence — and one winter it got so cold that admiral Bryd hurriedly left town to keep from catching double pneumonia. That was the day the Amarillo zoo's foremost attraction, a polar bear, froze to death.

How Dry Was It? It was so dry my pet duck was three years old before he learned to swim.

That's Thin During a drought, two cattlemen were talking. One asked, "How are things with you?"

The other replied, "Not good. My cattle are so thin that I'm using carbon paper and branding 'em three at a time."

How Windy Was It? The wind was blowing so hard that it knocked John Wayne off his horse at the drive-in movie.

Come Quick "Hurry down to the big road an' help my paw," said the little boy as he ran up to a cabin door.

"What's happened?" the settler wanted to know.

"He fell off the wagon into the mud."

"Is he in very deep?"

"He's plumb up to his ankles."

"Oh, well, he's not bad off then."

"But mister," the boy said, "he fell in head first."

How Hot Was It? It was so hot the tobacco chewers were spitting brown steam.

How Cold Was It? It was so cold, the power line froze and we couldn't get any electricity through it.

Another Texas Classic A giant flock of ducks were winging their way south for the winter when they stopped at a small lake in the panhandle. Well, those ducks where just resting up when a sudden norther struck. The temperature dropped so fast that the water in the lake froze almost instantly; the poor ducks were trapped when their little webbed feet were frozen solid in the ice.

It didn't take long for a couple of farmers to find out what happened and they called all their neighbors to let them know the duck harvest was about to begin. When the first farmers started arriving, the ducks were naturally scared and, all together, they started wildly flapping their wings. Now you should know that thousands of ducks flapping their wings all at once creates considerable power. In this case it was sufficient power. Just as the farmers were about to start killing the ducks, the flapping created enough power to lift those ducks, carrying the frozen lake with them. As the farmers watched in disbelief, the ducks flew away as a group, carrying a homemade iceberg with them.

Rest of the Story As those ducks continued to fly south, the ice gradually began to melt. By the time time the ducks reached south Texas, the ice was melting at such a rate it seemed to be raining. Thanks to those ducks, parts of Texas had their largest rainfall in years.

How Severe Was the Drought? The crops were so bad that the crows had to lie on their stomachs to eat the corn.

How Hot Was It? It was so hot we had to feed the chickens cracked ice to keep them from laying hardboiled eggs.

A Texas Classic A visitor in West Texas on a particularly windy day stopped in a gas station for fuel and struck up a conversation with the attendant. "Say," he asked, "does it blow like this all the time?"
"No," the attendant replied, "sometimes the wind turns around and blows from the other direction."

The visitor continued on his journey until lunchtime when he stopped in a cafe. Hoping to get the upper hand on the local waitress, he said, "I understand it doesn't always blow this way around here."

"That's right, mister," she said, "sometimes it blows like hell."

How Cold Was It? It was so cold that when I took a pot of boiling coffee off the campfire, there was a sheet of ice across the top and I had to break through it to pour myself a cup of hot coffee.

How Hot Was It? It was hotter than high school love in the back seat of a Buick.

How Dry Was It? It was so dry we had to irrigate the rivers.

During the War, a lot of servicemen were trained in Texas, many of them in West Texas. On a very windy day, a visiting general was conducting a surprise inspection. While he was checking the troops, a soldier came floating down through the air and landed in the middle of the field.

The general, irritated at the intrusion, demanded, "What are you doing practicing parachuting on such a windy day?"

"Sir," replied the recruit meekly, "I didn't come down in a parachute. I went up in a tent."

How Hot Was It? We don't know, the mercury in the thermometer evaporated.

How Dry Was It? It was so dry the lifeguards only had to know how to wade.

Who Could Blame Him? During the 1950 Texas Open golf tournament, a thunderstorm caused Sam Snead to miss a putt that would have given him a course record 62. Afterwards, Sam explained, "It was a-rainin and a-hailin, the people was a-runnin and a-screamin, and how in hell could I putt?"

How Hot Was It? It was so hot I got blisters — on my boots.

That old philosopher Az Tex has this advice: The only thing worse than a flooded living room is a flooded attic.

And Finally, How Hot Was It? It was so hot the centerfold in Playboy magazine took off her staples.

4

I'll Drink To That

**Mary had a little lamb,
what'll you have?**

Although some might disagree, it is absolutely not true that all Texans drink. There have been plenty of Texans who have lived their entire life and never allowed spirits of any sort to touch their lips. For those Texans who do drink, that is just fine with them because it leaves more for the drinkers. Whatever your personal preference, it is a fact that some, perhaps many or even most, Texans do drink, and therein lies the source of some special humor.

Proof Positive That Not All Texans Drink   In the late 1880s many sections of Texas were actively pursuing prospective new settlers. In one magazine for possible homesteaders, the following advertisement appeared: Not a saloon in Jones County. Do you know that we consider this the grandest thing that could be said in our favor? Not a saloon in Jones County. Does not that in one sentence speak volumes in favor of the morality and sobriety of our town and country?

Jones County, located in West Texas, is named for Anson Jones, a President of the Republic of Texas.

Perhaps the Oldest Texas Drinking Joke   A cowboy who had spent six months riding range had a powerful thirst, and when he got to town he aimed to quench it. After several hours in a saloon, he finally dashed out, sailed through the air, and landed squarely in the street. A bystander asked, "Are you hurt?"

"Naw," replied the cowboy, "but I'd sure like to meet up with the s.o.b. that moved my horse."

How's That Again?   Back in the days of the national prohibition experiment, Pat Neff was running for governor. One of his campaign promises was to make Texas so dry, "A man will have to prime himself to spit." He was elected. Of course not all Texans favored prohibition. One slogan used by anti-prohibition proponents was, "Texans prefer their whiskey in bond, not the barn."

If you drink, don't drive! Don't even putt

From the Texas Bumper Sticker Hall of Fame. Seen on a Mercedes in Highland Park, Texas.

Ain't it the Truth If you drink and are rich, you're an alcoholic; if you're poor and you drink, you're a drunk.

The old Texan hurried into the watering hole and said to the bartender, "Quick, give me a drink. I'm about to be in some big trouble."

The bartender poured the drink and the Texan downed it in one gulp. "Let me have another, quick. Boy, am I in trouble."

The bartender obliged and the Texan downed the drink. He slammed the glass on the bar and requested one more. As the Texan drank the third shot, the bartender couldn't contain his curiosity any longer. "Say fella," he said, "what kind a trouble are you gonna be in anyway?"

"You tell me," replied the Texan. "I don't have any money to pay for these drinks."

Join D.A.M.M. Drunks against Mad Mothers

From the Texas Bumper Sticker Hall of Fame. Seen on a pickup in Houston.

A Legendary Texas Drinker One of the most famous Texas drinkers was Bobby Layne, the all-American from the University of Texas that went on to a professional career before he retired to play golf, gin rummy, and poker in Lubbock. Some of the escapades attributed to Layne are actually a part of Texas folklore. Although Layne didn't necessarily deny the stories, he claimed he wasn't doing anything that everyone else wasn't doing except that he was man enough to go in the front door rather than slipping in the back where no one could see.

So widespread was Layne's reputation that comedian Bob Hope said Layne was the originator of the x-rated huddle and that his personal water bucket on the sideline always seemed to have a head on it.

One of the Layne stories occurred when he was playing for Detroit. Bobby was stopped for a traffic violation and the officer arrested him for being drunk on the grounds that his speech was slurred. Bobby beat that rap by convincing the judge that it wasn't alcohol that slurred his speech but rather his thick southern accent, something the policeman wasn't accustomed to hearing.

Perhaps the most famous Layne story supposedly happened before he even left Austin. It seems Bobby was driving home when several parked cars jumped out in front of him. At the trial, the arresting officer testified that Bobby could hardly talk when he was taken into custody. Bobby's attorney objected, claiming his client had simply had a bad case of laryngitis, to which the policeman replied, "What, a whole case?"

Wanna Have a Drink? The reputation of Texans liking their whiskey has been around for generations. The following, written by Alexander Edwin Sweet, appeared in an 1884 edition of *Texas Siftings*: "The typical Texan is a large-sized Jabberwock, a hairy kind of gorilla, who is supposed to reside on a horse. He is half alligator, half human, who eats raw buffalo, and sleeps out on a prairie. He is expected to carry four or five revolvers at his belt, as if he were a sort of preambulating gunrack. He also carries a large assortment of cutlery in his boot. It is believed that a failure to invite him to drink is more dangerous than to kick a can of dynamite."

A Drinking Classic Two old Texans had been friends for more years than they cared to count. Finally one of them was on his death bed and he called his friend to his side. "Look," he said, "I want you to do me one last favor. It looks like I won't get to use that quart of 12-year-old sipping whiskey I was saving for a special occasion. So when I'm gone, will you just pour it over my grave. It'll make me rest easier."

The friend hesitated for a moment than replied, "Well sure I'll do it, but since it won't make no difference to you, can I strain it through my kidneys first?"

Try It After a night of carousing and drinking, a sure way to drive your wife crazy is don't talk in your sleep, just grin.

That old philosopher Az Tex suggests: Never, ever, pour lots of black coffee down a drunk unless you want a wide-awake drunk on your hands.

CAUTION! Student Drinker!

From the Texas Bumper Sticker Hall of Fame.

Nice Try The drunk woke up with a severe headache and an angry wife. "Well dear," he said, "you should at least be proud of me because I didn't wake you when I came in last night."

"That's right you didn't," replied his wife. "But those two deputies who were carrying you sure did make a lot of noise."

A Texas Classic The traveler from New York was driving through Texas for the first time. He stopped for the night and registered in a motel. After checking in he asked the night clerk if he had any cigars. The clerk replied that he sure did and handed the visitor a stogie that was about the size of a fire hose.

"Isn't this a little large?" asked the traveler.

"Everything comes bigger in Texas," the clerk replied.

The New Yorker shrugged, lit up the cigar, and headed off to the bar smoking like the stack on a steam locomotive. Inside the saloon, he took a seat at the bar and ordered a cold beer. When it arrived it was the largest glass of brew the man had ever seen. "Isn't this a little large?" he asked.

"Everything comes bigger in Texas," the barkeep replied.

About the time he finished off the beer, the traveler realized it was time for an emergency run to the necessary room and he asked for directions. "Sure," replied the bartender pointing to a side exit, "through that door and turn left."

The man slipped off the stool and staggered through the exit but he unknowingly got the directions confused, turned right by mistake, and quickly found himself bobbing up and down in the motel swimming pool. Naturally, he commenced hollering for help immediately. A passerby heard the calls and went to the rescue. "Hurry up," pleaded the New Yorker, "Get me out a here before somebody flushes the damn thing."

Bad Beer Defined My definition of bad beer is that beer which is so bad that it ought to be poured back into the horse where it came from.

An Old Texas Saying Nothing makes a woman look as good as four or five cocktails in a man.

Second Oldest Texas Drinking Joke The old Texan lead an eventful life and he was always certain to start each day drinking at least one gourd full of whiskey. Finally, after living through more experiences than half a dozen men, the old Texan died just before his 102 birthday.

A neighbor discovered the body and notified the authorities. When the old maid down the street heard the news she replied. "So, the whiskey finally got him, eh."

If you drink, don't park.
Accidents cause people

From the Texas Bumper Sticker Hall of Fame. Seen on a pickup in West Texas.

Research Doesn't Lie A friend who claims he has done years of research, which I don't doubt, says he has finally identified the six stages of intoxication. According to him they are:

Stage 1: I'm interesting

Stage 2: I'm invisible

Stage 3: I'm rich

Stage 4: I can ride anything with hair

Stage 5: I can lick any man in the bar

Stage 6: I'm bulletproof

Another Legendary Texas Drinker Another famous Texas drinker was John Nance "Cactus Jack" Garner, the Uvalde native who rose all the way to vice president of the United States. After Garner retired and moved back to Texas, a friend once asked how he was getting along. Garner supposedly replied, "Fine. I ain't gettin' drunk but once a day."

Perhaps the best Garner story is the one about the time he was talking to Dan Blocker, the Texan who played Hoss Cartwright on Bonanza.

"Son," Garner said, "you know I'm a lot older than you but you can see I'm pretty well preserved." Blocker agreed and Garner continued, "I attribute my long life to a rule I made when very young and that I've kept all my life."

"What's that rule, sir?" Blocker supposedly asked.

"I never take a drink before 5 o'clock. It would be a good rule for you to follow, understand."

"Yes sir," Blocker replied.

Garner then added, "Say, what time is it by your watch?"

"It's half past nine in the morning," Blocker replied.

"Hell, boy," replied Garner, "it's four and a half hours past 5 o'clock. Lets have a drink."

A Texas Tragedy The stranger drove into the small south Texas town and noticed the flag on the courthouse flying at half mast. Since he hadn't heard any news, he stopped a local citizen and asked who had died.

"No one that I know of," replied the local citizen.

"Well how come the flag is flying at half mast then?" asked the stranger.

"Oh that," explained the local man, "we only got one saloon and it's run plum out a beer."

My nomination for worst ever drunk joke. The Texan, who had had quite a bit more than a little too much to drink, was trying to find his way back to the Adolphus Hotel in Dallas. Unfortunately, he stumbled into a Catholic church by mistake and wound up in the confessional. The priest heard the bell and came at once. He asked, "Do you wish to confess your sins?"

"Naw," the Texan replied, "That'd take too long."

"How may I help you?" the Priest asked.

"I was wondering," the drunk replied, "you got any toilet paper on your side?"

Honky Tonk Signs

Over the years, Texas honky tonks and saloons have proven to be a hotbed of some humor in signs. The most classic was a sign that hung on the wall of a frontier Texas saloon which read: "Don't shoot the piano player; he's doing the best he can." What follows are some more modern examples:

Drink here, 4 out of 5 accidents happen at home.

If you are drinking to forget, please pay in advance.

Not responsible for anything said after three beers.

Don't put all you eggs in one basket
or all your whiskey in one woman.

If you can't walk out of here, don't crawl.

Please do not drink more than you can walk out with.

Never forget that you are one of all of the
people who can be fooled some of the time.

Don't swear before ladies; let them swear first.

Mary had a little lamb, what will you have?

You don't have to be crazy to tend bar here, but it helps a lot.

Our whiskey makes you feel single and see double.

We put you in the best of spirits — and vice versa.

Even when you can't dazzle 'em with brilliance,
You can always baffle 'em with Bull Sheeeeeeit.

Don't try to keep up with the Joneses, they just might be newlyweds.

And my nomination for best ever Texas saloon sign is:

If your nerves are shot, don't reload with whiskey.

5

Black Gold or Fools Gold?

**Texas Oil,
good to the last drop.**

In 1901 oil was discovered in some salt domes near a place called Spindletop. It was the oil discovery that launched the liquid fuel age because, for the first time, petroleum was available in sufficient quantities to make fuel affordable. In the years that followed, there were many more large discoveries in Texas, including some huge finds in East Texas and in the Permian Basin of West Texas. So much oil was found that Texas quickly gained the reputation of being the land of millionaires. The result was a lot of humor (and some wisdom) about the oilmen and their riches. Here's a collection of some of the best.

So That's Their Secret Ever wonder what the secret is to making a lot of money in the oil business? Dallasite H. L. Hunt, who was probably the richest man in the world when he died, said "You have to be lucky." One of his sons, Ray Hunt, offered this advice: "Given the choice between luck and intelligence, always take luck." Sid Richardson, one of the most famous of all Texas oilmen said, "Luck has helped me every day of my life and I'd rather be lucky than smart 'cause a lot of smart people ain't eatin' right."

On the other hand, Hugh Roy Cullen, another famous Texas oilman, said, "If you plan anything before you do it, you will usually come out all right. When you jump into anything without thinking about it ahead of time, you've got to trust luck." He also said "The trouble with this business is everybody expects to find oil."

Houston oilman Thomas W. Blake may have put it all into perspective when he said, "What it comes down to is big time gambling with all the latest scientific helps." Thirty-dollar-a-barrel oil would also help.

Good Advice Oilman Ted Weiner had this advice for anyone considering an oil deal. "Anybody who's going to put money into an oil deal ought to find out two things. First, is he going to get a complete return on his investment before the operator starts taking a percentage? Second, is the operator putting in some money of his own? If both answers are affirmative, he's probably got the basis for a pretty fair deal." Sounds reasonable.

A Texas Classic Not long ago, a Texan hocked all he owned to buy a used Cadillac. He headed for New York to do a little bragging. By the time he got to Arkansas, he had three oil wells, two Cadillacs, and a race horse. Before he got out of Tennessee, he had a dozen oil wells and a Cadillac for each one, three racehorses, and one thousand head of cattle. As he went through the Carolinas his holding grew to one thousand oil wells with a refinery and a pipe line, a Cadillac dealership, a racehorse breeding farm and ten thousand head of cattle. By the time he reached New York, his life had settled down — he simply owned half the King ranch. According to J. Frank Dobie, many Texas fortunes were acquired in a similar fashion.

Good Motto FORTI ET FIDELI NIHIL DIFFICILE. From the coat of arms of legendary wildcatter Glen McCarty. Translated it means "For the brave and the faithful, nothing is impossible."

Bumper sticker seen in Houston: The world's worst four-letter word — OPEC.

The Little Woman The oilman's wife was so proud of herself. "Honey," she said to her husband, "I finished balancing the checkbook and the checks total the exact amount I'm overdrawn." That woman is living proof that she had more money than she could afford.

The Texas oilman, visiting New York for the first time, went into a bar and sat down alone. In a few minutes an attractive lady came in and sat down beside him. Naturally, being a gentleman, the Texan introduced himself. "Hello little darlin'," he said, "I'm Billy Fred Benson from . . . . "

"Don't tell me," the lady interrupted, "you're from Texas."

"Why yes," he said, "how did you know?"

"Well," the lady answered, "you're named Billy Fred, you called me darlin', and you seem so tall sitting there in that chair."

"Well you sure are perceptive," Billy Fred replied, "except for one thing."

"And what's that?" she asked.

"I'm not really tall," replied the Texan, "I'm just sitting on my wallet."

Texas Oilmen have a passion for large, sprawling houses. If you doubt that, take a drive through the River Oaks section of Houston where more than a few rich Texans hang their hat and a lot of them are oilmen. Of course, the problem is, all the rich folks in that neck of the woods tend to try to outdo one another when they build a house. And sometimes the houses get really large. One family had a house so large it required three mailboxes. Another was so large it required its own zip code on mail. But the largest of all was the house with an intercom system that had to have a separate area code.

The most famous Texas house story is the one about the oilman's wife who built a sprawling home in River Oaks and naturally had a party when it was finished to show off a little to the neighbors. When one guest asked how many bathrooms the home had, the lady simply answered, "Oh, I can seat seven."

A Texas Classic This is supposed to be a true story. An oilman's house caught fire one day down in Houston. The press covered the event and made note that the lady of the house was seen helping fight the fire while wearing her mink coat over a nightgown. A couple of days later the paper got a note from the lady informing them she was not wearing her mink coat to fight the fire. It was her sable coat.

From the So Would I Department Overheard at a bar in San Antonio, "I'd give a thousand dollars to be an oil millionaire." Maybe that explains the old Texas saying: A millionaire is nothing but a poor man with money.

College Graduate Then there was the oilman who had a daughter that was into hard rock so he bought her a petrified forest. When she grew up and graduated from the University of Texas, she received an M.B.A. — Massive Bank Account — from daddy.

To get along well, Dig it deep

From the Texas Bumper Sticker Hall of Fame. Seen on an oil well drilling truck near Odessa, Texas.

Roughneck Classic If it hadn't been for the roughnecks — the men willing to do the dirty work at the drilling site — there never would have been a Texas oil industry. The truth is, working on an oil well can be such a difficult job that someone once observed there were two requirements for becoming a roughneck: you had to have a strong back and a weak mind.

The roughnecks were frequently a poorly educated, hard-working class of men who didn't particularly care for anyone who did have an education. Geologists were a frequent target of roughneck humor and here is probably the most popular geologist joke:

A drilling contractor drove up to a well site one day in a new Cadillac convertible with a whore by his side and a one-horse trailer hooked on behind. "How's it going boys?" he asked.

"Just fine," replied the foreman, "we're down to the depth that the geologist claimed would be the pay-zone. Say, where is the geologist anyway?"

"Aw, I fired that s.o.b." replied the contractor.

"You fired the geologist!"

"Sure as hell did," said the contractor. "Now I got me a whore and a racehorse. And let me tell you boys, when compared to a geologist, one of 'em is more fun and the other is more reliable."

We Mean Rich Did you hear about the ultra rich Texan? He was buried in a three-room casket. When they read his will, it was revealed he had left his son only three million dollars. A note attached proclaimed, "He's damn lucky I didn't cut him off altogether."

That old philosopher Az Tex observed: If you drill enough oil wells you will eventually learn the sound of suckin' wind when you hit a dry hole.

Old Texas Oil Field Maxim: A gusher clouds a land title; a dry hole clears it.

Oldest of all Texas Oil Jokes The former Texas oilman died and went to heaven but he found the gate closed. When he asked why, St. Peter replied, "We already have an abundance of Texas oilmen in heaven and the way they are acting, we're afraid they will start drilling in the golden streets any moment."

The oilman though for a moment, then proposed a bargain. "St. Peter," he said, "if you'll let me in, I think I can solve your problem."

St. Peter decided to take a chance and let the man in on probation. The oilman immediately sought each Texas driller and whispered in his ear, "Did you hear they found a big new field down in Hell?"

Sure enough, one by one, the other oilmen packed up and headed for hell. When most were gone, St. Peter sought out the Texan to thank him and to ol' Pete's surprise he found that Texas oilman packing his bags.

"Why are you packing?" asked St. Peter.

"Well, it's this way," the Texan said. "There are so many drillers headin' south that I decided there might be something to this rumor, after all."

Most Famous Boomtown Joke In the oil boomtowns in Texas, mud was a legendary problem. In Mexia, a new arrival in town spied a brand new Stetson hat laying in the mud and bent over to retrieve it. To his shock, there was a man's head underneath. Startled, the stranger pulled back and exclaimed "Sorry, I didn't realize anyone was wearing the hat . . . Say are you ok down there?"

"Oh yeah," the man replied, "but I'm gettin' a little concerned about this horse I'm riding."

Second Most Famous Boomtown Joke A stranger came drifting into the boomtown and, even though alcohol was illegal, asked a local man if there was any place where a person could purchase some liquid refreshment to sooth a parched throat.

The local man pointed down the street and said, "You see that big building down the street on the corner?"

"Yeah, I see it," the stranger replied.

"Well," the man said, "that's the post office. You can't get a drink there or at the Baptist church."

How Was the Gravy? Food in Texas boomtowns was notoriously bad. Ned Alvord, an old-time circus press agent, may have put it all into perspective when he remarked during preparations for the 1936 Texas Centennial, "They're building monuments to Sam Houston when all he ever done was to face Mexican bullets on the battlefield; I ate in the cafes of Longview during the oil boom."

Thanks for the Memory Comedian Bob Hope, who dabbled in Texas oil, once swore he saw a Texas oil millionaire drop a quarter in a Miami, Florida hotel lobby. When a bell boy picked it up and handed it to him, the Texan said, "Thanks, pardner" and tipped him a dollar.

Second Oldest Texas Oil Joke The Texas oilman went down to take his drivers test and failed the eye test miserably. The DPS trooper explained he could not drive a car without wearing glasses. "But I can't stand wearing glasses," the oilman replied.

"Well, you don't have any choice," the Trooper replied.

"We'll see about that," replied the oilman and he left.

Two weeks later the oilman was back and ready to take his drivers test. "Where are your glasses?" asked the trooper.

"Don't need 'em," replied the oilman, "I had the windshield in my car ground to my prescription."

The Little Woman That same oilman's wife checked into the hospital for some minor surgery. When the anesthesiologist told her she was going to have a local anesthetic, she replied, "Oh, my husband can afford it, order something imported."

That old philosopher Az Tex observed: It's harder for a rich man to get into heaven or jail. Come to think of it, I don't remember a rich Texas oilman ever going to jail.

A Texas Classic The oilman was working a lot of hours and not taking care of himself as he knew he should. One morning he felt some sudden pains in his chest and decided he might be having a heart attack. Without hesitation, the oilman pressed the buzzer on his intercom and yelled to his secretary, "Don't just sit there, go buy me a hospital."

How Many? When Lamar Hunt got into the professional football business, his first year wasn't successful and he lost a million dollars on his then Dallas Texans. When Lamar's father, H. L. Hunt, was told of the loss, he commented, "Well, at that rate he can last about 150 years."

From the Texas Bumper Sticker Hall of Fame. Back in the early seventies, when the first oil crisis hit America, Texans were not at all pleased to be sitting in long gas lines when a considerable percentage of the nation's fuel was produced in Texas. This became a popular bumper sticker of the times.

Another classic from the Texas Bumper Sticker Hall of Fame that originated during the time of the oil crisis. A lot of Texans believed Texas would have been better off to secede from the Union rather than ship Texas gasoline and oil to the Yankees. Although it was not stated in so many words, the underlying feeling was, "let's secede and dare them to come and get our oil."

What, No Pool? The oilman called home and asked to speak to his wife. The maid said she was busy. "But I'm her husband, get her on the phone."

The maid resisted. "She can't come to the phone right now."

"Well why in the hell not?" demanded the oilman.

The maid hesitated and the oilman repeated his demand. Finally, the maid gave in, "Your wife is upstairs making love with the neighbor."

"The neighbor," screamed the oilman, "hell, he's my best friend."

"I'm sorry. You made me tell."

"OK, listen carefully. Here in Texas we know how to deal with unfaithful wives and friends . . . . You got to get my pistol and kill 'em both."

"I can't do that," the maid exclaimed.

"I'll give you a million dollars and hire the best lawyer money can buy to get you off. I guarantee no jury in Texas will convict you," the oilman explained.

"Where's the gun," asked the maid.

The oilman told her where it was and then listened. He heard the sound of a door crashing open and gunfire then he heard the sounds of smashing glass, furniture being turned over, and people running and several more shots. Finally the maid comes back on the line. "Well, it's done," she said, "I got 'em both. When do I get the money?"

"What was all the racket?" asked the oilman.

"Well, I got that hussey of a wife of yours right off while she was still in bed. But the neighbor, he broke and ran. I chased him down the stairs, through the game room, around the pool, and finally got him out near the statue in the garden."

There was a short pause. "Pool?" the oilman said, "We don't have a . . . say, what number is this anyway?"

Money Matters With all the money that has circulated in and through Texas, there have been some interesting observations by the men who seemed to have the most. One of the most famous quotes came from H. L. Hunt. He said, "Money is nothing. It is just something to make bookkeeping convenient."

Another famous Texan, Clint Murchison, once said, "Money is a lot like manure. Pile it up in one place and it stinks like hell. But spread it around and it does a lot of good." It was also Murchison who noted, "Cash makes a man careless."

Dallas oilman Ray E. Hubbard probably put the whole money question into perspective when he said, "Anybody that's got money can hire somebody who's smart to make them more money. It's the son of a bitch that hasn't got any money that has to be smart."

Another oilman explained his views with a sign he kept on his desk:

THERE IS NO SUCH THING AS PETTY CASH.

Cadillac Chronicles

One by-product of the oil riches in Texas was a legendary love affair that developed between wealthy Texans and the Cadillac automobile. The affair built to such proportions that Art Buchwald once commented, "Texas is the most Cadillac-conscious state in the Union." Naturally there have been a multitude of Texas Cadillac stories, many of them are actually true. A lot of people swear an oilman went to Dallas one time and actually charged a Cadillac to his hotel room. Down in Houston there really was, supposedly, an oilman who had a different colored Cadillac for each day of the week. Another Houston wildcatter supposedly had a different Cadillac for each direction he drove, although no one ever explained what he did if he was driving south and suddenly had to turn right.

Then there was the Houston oilman who traded Cadillacs everytime the ashtrays got full. But the most outlandish story about Cadillacs is the one where the rich Texas oilman bought his German shepherd his very own Cadillac to chase.

Stanley Marsh III, one of the few remaining eccentric Texas rich, once commissioned a Cadillac ranch out in the panhandle. He had several Cadillacs buried up to their windshield so anyone driving in from New Mexico would have some to look at.

Then there was the famous nursery thyme that was rewritten slightly for Texans. It went, "the butcher, the baker, the Cadillac maker . . ."

Another Texan supposedly went into a Cadillac dealership a few years ago and plunked down two $10,000 bills. When told that was more than enough, he replied, "Give me the change in Volkswagens." Two other rich Texans were out pricing Caddies. One of the men found a model he liked and asked how much.

"$15,000," the salesman replied.

"I'll take it," the Texan said and he reached for his wallet.

"No, No," his friend said, "You got breakfast. This is on me."

Of course all the Cadillac stories don't have happy endings. One Texan drove his $25,000 El Dorado to Las Vegas and came home in a $250,000 Greyhound.

Perhaps the most famous Texas Cadillac joke of all time was the one about the two rich Texans who finally decided to take up the game of golf. Naturally being rich, they hired a professional golfer to give them lessons. When the Texans showed up for lesson number one, the pro announced there would be a short delay since there were no caddies available.

"Well, don't you worry, son" said one of the Texans, "if we have to, we can use Buicks."

Things That Go Boom Also Go Bust!

Just as Texas and the Texans enjoyed the luxury provided by oil, so have both the state and her citizens suffered in the current price crunch. But through it all, Texans have somehow managed to hold onto their sense of humor. Today, oil field bust jokes are about as popular as oil jokes were in the good times. Here are some examples.

Check the Hood One result of the oil price collapse is that many Texans are being forced to keep their Cadillacs a little longer than usual. Some Texas families that once handed down Cadillacs like other families did clothes are actually being seen in models that are several years old. One oilman may have overdone it. He pulled into one of those garages that advertise a ten-minute oil change, and after the mechanic checked the engine, he advised, "Keep the oil, change cars."

Hard Times A sure sign of hard times in Texas — oilmen are wearing ten-quart hats.

That old philosopher Az Tex once observed that the trouble with Texas oilmen these days is that they have learned that a $30-a-barrel lifestyle just can't be supported by a $15-a-barrel price of oil.

What Do You Mean Overdrawn? Have you heard about the oilman's wife who thought she couldn't be overdrawn because she still had checks left.

Two old wildcatters were over in East Texas taking soil samples while trying to decide where to drill next. Sure enough, quite by accident, they found gold. One of the men remarked, "We really ought to remember where this place is in case the price of oil ever falls." At last report, those two oilmen were digging up half of East Texas trying to find that gold mine.

Jane Doe These days, people in the oil industry are having to put in some long hours trying to rebuild their fortunes. In Midland, one oilman's wife claims her husband has been gone so much lately that if she died, he wouldn't be able to identify the body.

Happy Days A Texas oilman died and willed what was left of his once vast fortune to the two women most responsible for his years of peace and happiness — two old girlfriends who had each refused his proposal of marriage.

Wedded Blisters There was an oilman down in Houston who gave his wife plastic surgery — he cut up her credit cards. Soon afterwards she lost 200 pounds — divorced her husband. Unfortunately the divorce had to be annulled because neither one wanted the kids. In an unrelated case, another oilman's wife became disgusted with her husband for never making any money so she divorced him. Unfortunately, her former husband quickly fell behind in his child support payments and she had to repossess him.

Texas Riddle No. 2: Do you know the difference between a bird and a Texas oilman? See last page for answer.

A Modern Fairy Tale Two woman were walking through the woods, going to grandma's house, when they came upon a frog. The slimy creature looked up at one of the girls and pleaded, "If you will kiss me, I will turn into a Texas oilman."

The young lady studied the frog for a moment then bent down, picked him up, and put him gently into her purse. "Aren't you going to kiss him?" asked her friend.

"Hell no," the woman replied, "These days a talking frog is worth a lot more than a Texas oilman."

Texas Riddle No. 3: Do you know the difference between the Titanic and the Texas oil business? See last page for answer.

That old philosopher Az Tex has observed that the only thing Texas oilmen are taking in the Permian Basin these days is a bath.

A Perplexing Question Which of the following do not fit: gonorrhea, herpes, AIDS, and a house in Houston? Gonorrhea. It's the only thing on that list you can get rid of.

Sounds Right Someone has suggested that the best exploration team in the world these days is the Sears credit department in Midland, Texas.

Texas Riddle No. 4: What do Dolly Parton, Morgana the kissing bandit, and a Texas oilman have in common? If you don't know, see the answer page in back.

The fat lady is singing in Midland, Texas

Chapter 11 in '87

These two members of the Texas Bumper Sticker Hall of Fame were seen in Midland, Texas during the height of the oil price crisis.

The Little Woman Strikes Again A lot of Texas oilmen went totally broke when the price crunch hit a few years ago, but one operator down in Houston managed to salt away a small sum before the bottom fell out. He could have gotten by for some time if his wife hadn't come home one day loaded down with packages marked Neiman Marcus. She announced, "Honey, I have great news. Our nest egg hatched."

Texas Riddle No. 5: Do you know how to become a Texas oil millionaire these days? See last page for answer.

That old sage Az Tex believes that the best way to rob a Texas bank these days is to own it. That may explain why a lot of Texas banks that once issued oil loans are now issuing insufficient fund notices on themselves. It may also explain why, in most Texas financial institutions, NO has become a complete sentence.

Last Request The Houston oilman had a heart attack and died. His last request was that his favorite bankers act as pall bearers. "They've carried me for the last three years," he said, "so they might as well finish the job."

Did It Hurt? Did you hear about the Houston oilman's wife who was dismembered? She was kicked out of the River Oaks Country Club.

How's That Again? Overheard in a Houston bar: "I'm going down to the bank tomorrow to see if I can't borrow enough money to get out of debt." Which brings to mind the old Texas saying, "Isn't it a shame that the man who writes the ads for the banks doesn't also write the loans."

A Change of Pace It would appear that it will be some time, if ever, before the good old days of quick oil fortunes return. As a result, a lot of Texans are now seeking their fortunes in more conventional ways, like working for it. If you fall in this category, you might need some help. Here's a twelve-step plan, developed by Billie Sol Estes, that might help:

1. Get up early, plan your day positively. Do something good for each person you see. A sense of humor is essential.

2. Have faith in yourself and your business deal. Get a deal that will work and make money, and then others will join you. You won't have to find people — they will find you.

3. Get good legal and accounting advice.

4. Hire the best people available. They will make you money. Delegate to others what they do better than you.

5. Have zeal and enthusiasm. Start a fire within you. Some will come join you, others will watch you burn.

6. Be original and mysterious. Don't try to be like everyone else; hold back a part of yourself. Don't tell all of your innermost thoughts and feelings.

7. Share yourself. Love your fellow man. Cast your bread upon the waters. You will multiply by dividing.

8. Be competitive. That's the American way. Get in the last lick. He who laughs last does laugh best.

9. Live life to the fullest, a day at a time, and make each day your best.

10. Take risks and borrow to the limit to back your ventures. The best fruit is at the end of the limb.

11. Learn from your failures. Forgive the past and at all costs, keep moving.

12. Be willing to listen, be ready, and when the big play arrives, recognize it and go for it with all you've got.

Good luck!

6

Law and Disorder

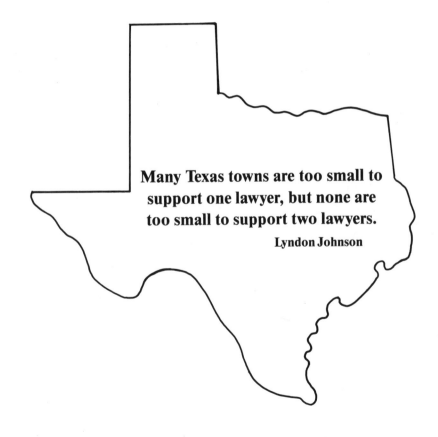

Many Texas towns are too small to support one lawyer, but none are too small to support two lawyers.

Lyndon Johnson

Someone once said that Texas is a two-sport state, football and spring football. That's not exactly accurate. Texas may just be a three-sport state. After football and spring football comes making fun of the law and lawyers. It has been suggested that one reason law humor is so popular is that if you ever get into a battle of wits with one of those gents (or gentettes) that practice law for a living, you are almost always dealing with an unarmed person. Here's a collection of some law and disorder Texas humor.

How Much Per Pound? A friend swears he received the following from his attorney: For services rendered. Total bull $500.

Now That's Fast This is said to have happened in a Dallas courtroom. The prosecuting attorney had done his job well and was pleased when the jury returned the verdict of "guilty as charged." Unfortunately the judge saw fit to be unreasonably lenient when he passed sentence. The prosecutor objected sternly.

"What do you base your objection on?" asked the judge.

"On the grounds, sir, that with the parole laws, possible time off for good behavior, and the early release program, the defendant will probably beat the jury home."

Rest of the Story The lawyer was so mad he just kept arguing the case and wouldn't shut up. Finally 'hizzoner' had had enough. "If you keep arguing this case, I'll find you in contempt of court," the judge warned.

"Your honor," the lawyer said, "I'm not arguing the case; I'm just cussing your stupid decision." No one has seen that lawyer in years.

Medical Advancement The dean of the science department down at Rice University recently announced they were switching from white rats to lawyers for their experiments. When asked why, the dean explained: "We switched to lawyers for three reason. First, there's more of 'em than rats; second, you don't get attached to lawyers; and finally, there are some things a white rat just won't do.

DON'T TELL MOM I'M A LAWYER
SHE THINKS I'M A PIANO PLAYER
IN A WHOREHOUSE!

From the Texas Bumper Sticker Hall of Fame.

That old philosopher Az Tex believes he has found the reason lawyers are so hard to get along with. They believe the best things in life are fees.

Oldest of All Lawyer Jokes The pleasure boat ran aground just off the Texas coast. There was some panic because, even though the ship was close to shore, the waters were teeming with man-eating sharks. Even though it was risky, someone had to chance a swim to shore to get help. Finally an auto mechanic out of Dallas volunteered. He dove in the water and swam about 100 yards before the sharks ate him. A Baptist preacher volunteered next and he made it about 50 yards before becoming dinner for the sharks. Three other men tried it but all failed to make more than fifty yards before the sharks attacked.

When everyone was about to give up, a lawyer out of Houston dove into the water and swam safely all the way to shore. Two men who were standing on the ship deck saw it happen with their own eyes. "It's a miracle," one said.

"Naw it wasn't," countered the other.

"Well how do you explain it?" asked the first.

"Simple, those sharks let the lawyer go through out of professional courtesy."

The single most perplexing question facing mankind is why on earth a lawyer's brief is called a brief.

There's an old saying, you can't take it with you, which is true. But if enough lawyers are involved in settling your estate, you can't leave it behind either.

Surely you've heard about the Dallas lawyer who taught his children the alleged facts of life. He's the same lawyer who is willing to spend your last dollar to prove he's right, which proves the point that practicing law doesn't make you perfect, only rich.

It's a Little Late The lawyer was sick — very sick — and not expected to live. A friend went to visit and found the lawyer hurriedly thumbing through the Bible. "Well," said the friend, "it's about time you got some religion."

"Religion, hell," replied the lawyer, "I'm looking for loopholes."

Rest of the Story That lawyer finally promised God that if He would spare him, he'd be good the rest of his life. That poor lawyer, who did recover, spent all his remaining days searching for loopholes in the ten commandments.

Are They Bicuspids? While it's true some Texas laws have teeth, very few of them are wisdom teeth.

It has been proven time and time again that the hardest laws to live with are in-laws.

One reason lawyers are unpopular is that so many people only believe in law and order when they can lay down the law and give the orders.

Sad But True A lawyer is only as good as his last case.

Best Excuses If you travel much through Texas and happen to get a traffic citation in one of the rural areas, you will get to meet someone called the justice of the peace. A contributor spent several years working for a local JP and carefully recorded some of the best excuses used in a vain attempt to beat a traffic ticket. Here's her top ten list of all-time favorites:

Number 10: "I was almost out of gas and I was trying to get to a station as fast as I could."

Number 9: "I was speeding because the baby needed changing and I couldn't stand the smell."

Number 8: "I had to speed. My girlfriend needed to go to the bathroom."

Number 7: "I didn't know the light was red. I'm color blind."

Number 6: "I was trying to get off the radar screen."

Number 5: "Gee, I didn't even know there were that many miles in an hour."

Number 4: "I was running late for a funeral."

Number 3: "I had just washed my car and I was trying to air dry it."

Number 2: "I left my bra at my boyfriend's house."

And the Number 1 all-time excuse for speeding: My wife called and said she wanted to get pregnant. This was selected number one because it's the only one that worked.

So You Thought the State of Texas Cared? A motorist once purchased a new car and left immediately on a trip. Although he was careful to set his speedometer at exactly the speed limit, he was stopped for speeding within ten miles. He tried to explain to the trooper that he wasn't speeding but was told to tell it to the judge. The man continued his trip but stopped at the next town and had his speedometer checked. Sure enough it was defective and the dealer fixed it immediately. The motorist confidently wrote the judge a letter and explained his predicament. He enclosed a copy of the repair order that he anticipated would be sufficient proof of his claim. In a week he received the following one-line reply: The state of Texas doesn't even care if you have a speedometer, $65.00.

The lawyer idly pitched a package of gum up in the air as he cross-examined a policeman in a trial where a man was accused of running a stop sign.

"What did you observe?" asked the lawyer.

"I saw the defendant go through the stop sign without coming to a complete stop."

"And how far away were you?" asked the lawyer while he continued to pitch the pack of gum up into the air.

"About half a block, sir," replied the policeman.

"And from that distance you could tell he didn't actually stop."

"I could," said the traffic cop.

"Well, maybe you could help me then," said the lawyer. "As you know when I pitch this pack of gum up, it eventually comes to a stop and then falls back. Now you're a lot closer than half a block away so I wonder, officer, can you see exactly when this gum stops before it falls back?"

Case dismissed.

That old philosopher Az Tex once observed: The sure by-product of man's inhumanity to his fellow man is lawyers.

Perfect Logic The Texas Rangers (the lawmen, not the baseball players) have been rounding up bad guys since before Texas became an independent Republic. One of the most famous rangers of all time, Lone Wolf Gonzaulles, once killed a suspect. There was some talk that Lone Wolf might have to stand trial. When asked about it he replied, "I'd rather be tried for killing a dozen s.o.b's in enforcing the law than have one of them tried for killing me."

It was Davy Crockett, perhaps the most famous adopted son of Texas, who once said law ought to be based on "the principles of common justice between man and man" and "natural born sense" and not on "law learning." It'll never happen, Davy.

That old philosopher Az Tex once observed: Many lawyers know as much about the law as a $2 hooker does about love.

There's an old Texas saying that practicing law may not be the oldest profession, but the results to the client are the same.

It'll Work Everytime Did you hear about the photographer assigned to take a picture of the graduating class from the Law School at the University of Texas? He got everyone to smile at the same time when he encouraged them to "Say fees."

White or Wheat? It was also LBJ who once said at a meeting of U.S. attorneys, "Lawyers are like bread — they are best when they are young and fresh."

Greyhound or Trailways? Perhaps the most famous Texas quote concerning the legal profession came from Lamar Hunt, owner of the Kansas City Chiefs and son of the famous H. L. Hunt. Lamar Hunt, who was actively involved in the NFL lawsuit to try to prevent Al Davis from moving his Oakland Raiders to Los Angeles, commented after the trial, "The best description of utter waste would be for a busload of lawyers to go over a cliff with three empty seats."

That old philosopher Az Tex once observed: The more lawyers involved, the longer the case.

Good Motto A not so famous Dallas lawyer once had a sign hanging on his wall proclaiming in Latin, Suum Cuique, which translates as "To every man, his own." One of his clients saw the sign and commented, "'Sue 'um quick' — that's a damn good motto for a lawyer."

A Sure Sign A stranger moved into a West Texas town and was seen walking down the street one day. "Who's the stranger?" a cowboy asked another.

"I dunno," his friend replied, "but he ain't no lawyer — he's got his hands in his own pockets."

Theft Proof As you may or may not know, the Texas state capitol is the largest state capitol in the United States. In fact, it is even larger than the national capitol in Washington, DC. Many people assume the capitol was built so large because in Texas, everything is built bigger and better. As far as the capitol is concerned, it had to be built that big to keep the politicians and lawyers from stealing it.

Wrong Number A young attorney was sitting in his office on the first day he opened his practice. He was surprised to see a man walking into the office so soon after he opened, so the lawyer grabbed the phone and began speaking as if he were talking to a client. "Yes, sir," the lawyer said into the phone, "I'll handle that merger for you. Why sure I can help you incorporate, after all, I've been practicing business law for years and years." When he hung up the phone, the lawyer looked at the man who had come into his office. "You know us lawyers," he said, "busy, busy, busy. But I always have time for one more client, So tell me what can I do for you?"

"Nothing," the man replied, "I'm just here to install the phone."

Boy or Girl? That same young attorney was working on his first case down in Houston. He walked into court one morning and boldly asked the judge for a continuance.

"On what grounds?" asked the judge.

"Well, your honor," the lawyer said, "the defendant in this case had a baby this morning."

"I see," said the judge, "well how long of a continuance do you suppose she will need?"

"Oh, not more than a day or two," replied the attorney, "it was just a little tiny baby.

You surely have heard about the Texan who died and went to heaven. The other souls who lived behind the pearly gates didn't think anyone who lived in heaven on earth ought to get the same privilege after death so they decided to file an injunction with St. Peter to keep the Texan out. They would have done it, too, if they could have just found a lawyer to handle the paper work.

Surely you have heard about the burglar who was too poor to afford his own attorney. The judge asked, "Would you like the court to appoint an attorney for you?"

"No, your honor," replied the defendant, "I'll just throw myself on the ignorance of the court." That was twenty years ago and the burglar hasn't been heard from since.

It has been said in Texas that a good lawyer will know the law but the best lawyer will know the judge. Toward achieving that, a young lawyer found out that a certain judge liked to deep-sea fish so he invited the judge to spend the weekend out on the gulf. The only problem was, the young lawyer was prone to getting seasick; and sure enough, they hadn't been gone an hour when the lawyer became deathly ill. "Is there anything I can do?" asked the judge.

"It would help a lot," replied the lawyer, "if you'd overrule the motion."

How's That Again? The lawyer advised his client, "You are in a pretty tough spot. You'd better have an ironclad alibi or you're liable to hang."

"What's an alibi?" asked the defendant.

"That's where you prove you were somewhere else when you stole the car."

According to that old philosopher Az Tex: Old lawyers never die, they just lose their appeal.

The Jury Was in a Tough Spot The richest man in town was on trial charged with manslaughter in the death of his wife, who was not well liked in the community. The lawyer for the defense secretly assured the jury members they would be handsomely rewarded for an innocent verdict. The only problem was that while the jury sure wanted the reward, the evidence was overwhelming. Finally, after three days of deliberation the jury reached a verdict. They collected the handsome reward by finding the defendant not guilty on the grounds he had killed his wife so it couldn't be manslaughter.

Tell it to the Judge There was once an old-time gentleman who served as judge for a South Texas county. Whenever a lady was to appear as a witness, the judge would always say: "The lady will state her age, then be sworn."

That's Pure For his *Texas Proud and Loud,* Boyce House collected perhaps the best description of a defendant ever uttered in a Texas courtroom. The attorney shouted, "Gentlemen of the jury, my client is as pure as the dew-drop that sparkles on the tail of a Texas bull as he rises from his grassy couch and bellows in the face of the rising sun!"

Justice Will Be Done One of the most famous cases in Texas history involved a blacksmith charged with murder. When the jury returned a guilty verdict and ordered the man hung, the town had a problem — they only had one blacksmith and a lot of horses that needed shoeing. The city leaders finally resolved the issue by hanging the man's lawyer since they had plenty of lawyers.

Justice is Still Served The lawyer was all distraught. Despite his best efforts, his client was convicted and sentenced to death. When all appeals failed, the end appeared near for the client; but the lawyer had one more trick up his sleeve.

He approached the judge with an unusual deal. Since Texas uses lethal injection, the lawyer suggested his client be given a lethal injection of the deadly AIDS virus so he could then be used for medical research. He argued that his client would still be just as dead, but he would have a chance to contribute to society.

The judge gave the matter some serious consideration and finally agreed. On the appointed day, at the appointed time, the prisoner received the deadly injection. No sooner was the needle out, than the lawyer began to laugh hysterically. "What's so funny?" asked the judge.

"Boy, did we fool you," the lawyer said, "my client is wearing a condom."

20-20 Vision The attorney demanded severely, "You testify that you saw the defendant strike the complaining witness and yet you were three blocks away. How far can you see anyhow?"

"Oh, I don't know," the witness drawled, "about a million miles, I expect — say how far away is the moon anyway?"

Perhaps you thought it is up to the jury to determine guilt or innocence. Not true, the jury decides which side had the best lawyer.

A Fair Verdict Out in West Texas, they had an unusual case once. A deadbeat ran out on his wife and left her alone to fend for half a dozen kids. When the poor woman ran out of food, she was forced to steal a cow from the large herd of a neighbor in order to try to feed her children. Naturally, she got caught and was brought to trial. When the woman told her sad story to the jury, they felt pity for her, but she had admitted stealing the cow. After several hours of deliberation, the jury finally found a solution. They acquitted the woman on the grounds she had stolen the cow in self-defense.

The Rest of the Story Several years later, after the woman had struggled to raise the kids and make a life for herself, oil was discovered on her property and she became rich. Sure enough, about the time the woman was on easy street, her long lost husband showed up wanting his share of the loot. The woman reacted properly; she shot him between the eyes. When the case came to trial, the woman was convicted, but her lawyer managed to get her a suspended sentence. He convinced the jury to feel sorry for her because she was a widow.

Things That Go Boom in the Night One early Texas law that was difficult to enforce was the statue against fence-cutting. Hundreds of thousands of dollars were lost to the midnight callers who carried a pair of fence cutters and rode fast horses. The legislature tried to stop the crimes by making fence-cutting a felony, but still the wires got snipped with alarming regularity. Finally in desperation, the famed Texas Rangers were put on the case. One ranger, Ira Aten of the famous Frontier Battalion of Rangers, was sent to the area around Corsicana to stop the fence-cutting. He tried everything but nothing worked. Finally, using some good ol' Texas ingenuity, Ira came up with a plan as he explained in a letter to his Captain dated October 8, 1888.

Dear Sir,

I have only one more chance with any hopes of stopping fence-cutting in this section & that is with my dynamite boom as I call it. I have have had the law examined & it don't say any-thing about a man having the right to protect his property by the use of dynamite or by the use of a shot-gun either. So I have come to the conclusion if it was not against the law to guard a fence with a shotgun to protect the property, it certainly would not be against the law to use dynamite for the same purpose. There-fore I have invested some money in dynamite & will in a few day's set my dynamite boom's upon the few fences that have been put up recently to protect them. Should the Gov. or the Genl. disapprove of this, all they have got to do is notify me to the effect, &c. They sent me here to stop fence-cutting any way I could, & to use my own judgement &c, how to do it. And that is what I am doing & if they will let me alone the balance of the month I will have my boom's set & and when the fence is cut, why they will hear of it in Austin . . .

Don't be uneasy about my actions for I will use the greatest precaution with my boom's & see that no innocent men get's hurt with them. They are dangers in setting them unless a man is awful careful. How-ever, if I get blowed up, you will know I was doing a good cause . . . .

> You'r Very Respt.
> Ira Aten
> Co. 'D' Ranger

Unfortunately, Ira never explained exactly how his "booms" were going to work and there is no record of any fence cutters being blown to kingdom come for carrying out their handiwork.

A rich man was accused of murder and the evidence at the examining trial was very serious — so serious that not only did friends employ one of the leading lawyers in the state but the defendant's nephew slipped around to a prospective juror and said, "Johnson, if you get on that jury and make a successful fight for a verdict of manslaughter, I'll pay you a thousand dollars."

The man agreed and, in due course, was selected on the jury. After the testimony was concluded, the attorney for the defendant made a brilliant speech, which left the courtroom ankle-deep in tears.

It took three days and nights, but the jury finally came in with a verdict of manslaughter and a recommended term of four years in the penitentiary.

After the trial was over the nephew handed the juror the grand and said, "You earned it all right."

The man said, "Your darn tootin' I did! Those eleven other fools wanted to turn him a loose."

Then there was the man being tried for stealing a horse. He managed to get one the county's best lawyers who did a masterful job convincing the jury of his client's innocence. When the jury returned the not guilty verdict, the defendant was elated but confused. He asked while still in the courtroom, "Does this mean I get to keep the horse?"

A True Story The following story appeared in the May 15, 1885 issue of an El Paso newspaper under the headline A SLAP ON THE HAND: "Jesse Baskes was found guilty Monday of horse stealing and was sentenced to eleven years in the penitentiary. It looks like we're beginning to get soft."

Judge Roy Bean The most colorful man ever to dispense justice in Texas was Judge Roy Bean, the self-styled "Law West of the Pecos." Bean started out as a merchant in San Antonio, but he was run out of town when some of his customers found minnows swimming in their milk and didn't believe Roy when he claimed his cows had been drinking from a nearby creek.

Following his departure from the Alamo city, Roy settled in Langtry, Texas and with the help of some Texas Rangers got himself appointed justice of the peace. Armed with a copy of the 1873 *Revised Texas Statutes*, Judge Bean set about taming the wild frontier. Some of his decisions have become Texas legends:

Judge Roy once fined a corpse $40 for carrying a concealed weapon.

He once freed a man because there was nothing in his book of statues indicating it was against the law to kill a Chinaman.

After losing an election, the judge refused to leave office, proclaiming "Once a justice of peace, always a justice of peace."

When the judge had made up his mind on a case and announced his decision, he always said, "By gobs, that's my ruling."

When the governor of Texas tried to get Roy to give an accounting of his court, Bean replied: "Dear Governor. You run things up in Austin and I'll run things down here. Sincerely, Roy Bean."

"Water is the one thing people don't drink around here," was Judge Bean's reply when rejecting the offer of a water fountain from his idol, Lily Langtry.

Judge Roy Bean's ending for wedding ceremonies was simple: "I pronounce you man and wife. May god have mercy on your soul."

In any trial, the first question Bean felt had to be answered was: "Should the deceased have departed in the first place?"

One of Judge Roy Bean's actual written decisions: The deceased, unknown, came to his death at the hands of some person unknown who was a damned good shot.

ARGUMENTUM ADJUDICUM was Judge Roy Bean's motto. He translated it to mean "Don't argue with the judge." Very few people ever did.

TEMPLE HOUSTON

One of the most famous Texas lawyers of all time was Temple Houston, the son of Sam Houston and the first baby born in the Texas governor's mansion. In addition to practicing law, Temple was an accomplished gunman. Although probably not true, the story persists that Temple once caused Billy the Kid to withdraw from a shooting contest after witnessing a Temple Houston demonstration of true firearm skill. Temple served as a model for Edna Ferber's novel *Cimmarron.*

For all he did, Temple Houston was best known as an attorney. One of his most famous cases happened in Woodward, Oklahoma on Friday, May 25, 1899. Temple volunteered to defend one Minnie Stacey on the charges of running a bawdy house and plying her trade. Houston volunteered for the job and was given 10 minutes to prepare. His summation to the jury has become legend.

"Gentlemen, you heard with what cold cruelty the prosecution referred to the sins of this woman, as if her condition were of her own preference. The evidence has painted you a picture of her life and surroundings. Do you think they were of her own choosing? Do you think she willingly embraced a life so revolting and horrible? Ah, No! Gentlemen, one of our own sex was the author of her ruin, more to blame than she; then let us judge her gently. What could be more pathetic than the spectacle she presents? An immoral soul in ruin — where the star of purity once glittered, shame has set its seal forever, and only a moment ago they reproved her for the depths of which she had sunk, the company she kept, the life she led. Now, what else is left her? Where can she go and her sin not pursue her?

"Gentlemen, the very promises of God are denied her. He said: 'Come unto me all ye that labor and are heavy laden and I will give you rest.' She had indeed labored and is heavy laden, but if at this instant she were to kneel down before us all and confess her Redeemer and beseech his tender mercies, where is the church that would receive her? And even if they accepted her, when she passed the portals to worship and claim her rest, scorn and mockery would greet her and those she met would gather around them their skirts the more closely, to avoid the pollution of her touch. Would you tell me a single employment where she can realize?

"Give us this day our daily bread? Our sex wrecked her once pure life — her own sex shrink from her as they would the pestilence. Society has reared its relentless walls against her, and only in the friendly shelter of the grave can her betrayed and broken heart ever find the redeemer's promised rest. They told you of her assumed names, as fleeting as the shadows on the walls, of her sins, her habits, but they never told you of her sorrows, and who shall tell what her heart, sinful though it may be, now feels.

"When the remembered voices of mother and sisters, whom she must see no more on this earth, fall like music on her erring soul and she prays God that she could only return, and must not — no, not in this life, for the seducer has destroyed the soul. You know the story of the prodigal son, but for the prodigal daughter there is no return. Were she with her wasted form and bleeding feet, to drag herself back to home, she, the fallen and the lost, what would be her welcome? Oh, consider this when you come to decide her guilt; for she is before us, and we must judge her. They sneer and scoff at her. One should respect her grief, and I tell you, there reigns over her penitent and chastened spirit of desolation now that none, no, none, but the searcher of all hearts can ever know.

"None of us are utterly evil, and I remember that when the Saffron Scourge swept over the city of Memphis in 1878, a courtesan there opened wide the doors of her gilded palace of sin to admit the sufferers; and when the scythe of the reaper swung fast and pitiless she was angelic in her ministering. Death called her in the midst of her mercies and she went to join those she tried to save. She, like those the Lord forgave, was a sinner, and yet I believe that in the day of reckoning her judgement will be lighter than those who persecute and seek to drive off the earth such poor unfortunates as she whom you are to judge.

"They wish to fine this woman and make her leave. They wish to wring from her the wages of her shame the price of this mediated injustice; to take from her the little money she might have: and God knows, Gentlemen, it came hard enough. The old Jewish law told you that the price of a dog nor the hire of such as she should not come within the house of the Lord, and I say unto you that our justice fitly symbolized by a woman's form, does not ask at your hands the pitiful privilege of being left alone.

"The Master while on earth, while he spoke in wrath and rebuke to the kings and rules, never reproached one of these. One He forgave, another he acquitted. You remember both, and now looking upon this friendless outcast if any of us can say unto her, 'I am holier than thou' in the respect with which she is charged with sinning, who is he? The Jews who brought the woman before the Savior have been held up to the execration of the world for two thousand years. I always respect them. A man who will yield to the reproaches of his conscience as they did has the elements of good in him, but the modern hypocrite has no such compunctions. If the prosecutors of this woman whom you are trying had but brought her before the Savior they would have accepted his challenge and each gathered a rock and stoned her in the twinkling of an eye.

"No, Gentlemen, do as your Master did twice under the very circumstances that surround you. Tell her to go in peace."

She was acquitted as soon as the jury retired. Despite the claims of some, no record exists that she ever practiced her trade again.

7

Elected Humor

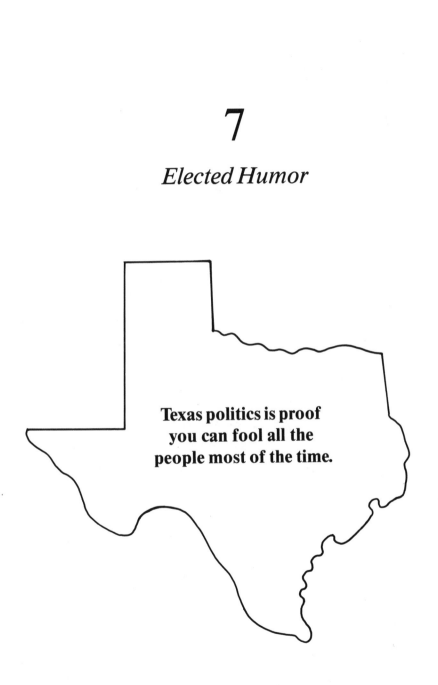

**Texas politics is proof
you can fool all the
people most of the time.**

One of the most popular "sports" in Texas is poking fun at politicians. A friend once suggested that Texans must like political jokes because they keep electing so many of them to office. His wife contradicted him, however, by saying that politics in Texas was nothing but a joke. Either way, here's a collection of some Texas political wit and wisdom.

That old philosopher Az Tex once observed: There ought to be a law in Texas that no more than two people can run for an office at the same time. If more than two run, it makes it too hard to pick the lesser of two evils.

Oldest and Best Texas Political Joke A young farm girl was out milking the family cow one day when a stranger approached and asked to see her mother.

"Mama," the young lady called out, "there's a man here to see you."

The mother looked out the kitchen window and replied, "Haven't I always told you not to talk to strangers. You come in this house right now."

"But mama," the little girl protested, "this man says he is a United States senator."

"In that case," the mother replied, "bring the cow with you."

Texas Logic The most dishonest man in the county was running for the state senate. And even though everyone knew he was dishonest, he was still elected. When the local head of the democratic party was asked to explain how such a man could be sent to Austin, he explained, "Well, it's this way. Anyone going into politics is bound to be corrupted sooner or later. So if we send one that is already corrupt, we don't spoil any of the good men in the county."

Second Oldest Texas Political Joke A candidate for the U.S. Senate was giving a stump speech in a small Texas town. A local school teacher thought the children might enjoy seeing a real politician so she turned out school and took the kids to hear the speech. The kids were all excited and little Bubba couldn't wait to get home to tell his father about the adventure.

"Did he speak all afternoon?" asked his father.

"Pert near," answered the boy.

"Well, what did he have to say?"

"I don't remember his exact words," Bubba replied, "but he sure did recommend himself highly."

That old philosopher Az Tex once observed: The cheaper the politician, the more he costs Texas.

Now That is Confidence There is lots of speculation about who will replace Bill Clements as governor of Texas. Will it be Ann Richards, Bill Mattox, Clayton Williams, Bill Hobby, or perhaps the legendary corporate raider T. Boone Pickens out of Amarillo. When asked about the possibility of his running, Pickens replied, "There's no one in Texas better prepared than I am to be governor. If I run for it, I want it. If I want it, I get it. And if I get it, I'll be the best damn governor ever." We'll see.

The size of Texas makes it difficult for those running for state office to cover all the ground, and even if they could, some of the ground is fearful to tread on. In the mid-1960s one unsuccessful candidate explained his loss with, "I went out into West Texas and was never heard of again."

Texas don't need no Sissy for a governor!

From the Texas Bumper Sticker Hall of Fame. Seen in Dallas when Francis "Sissy" Farenthal was running for governor.

Gibberish The Speaker of the Texas House of Representatives, Gibb Lewis, seems to have his way of talkin' which can be amusing. Once when he was confused about a particular issue, Mr. Speaker explained, "There's a lot of uncertainty that's not clear in my mind." When the Congress was working on the difficult problem of balancing the Texas state budget, Mr. Lewis advised it was necessary to "not only cut out the fat, we cut out a lot of meat." Concerning approval of his new budget approach he suggested, "run it up the flagpole and see who salutes that booger."

The subject of a pay raise for congressmen is always a touchy subject to the voters. Mr. Lewis, however, tried to put it into perspective by explaining that when you consider the entire state budget, a congressional pay raise amounted to nothing more then "a pimple on a frog." When a reform package for the criminal justice system was being considered, the Speaker assured its "ramifistations" would extend into the "hilterland." To Mr. Lewis, innuendoes are often any-u-windows and abnormal is occasionally adnormal, but he does believe that "prewarned is prearmed." On the subject of gun control, Gibb explains, "If there is one thing Texans care about, it's their First Amendment rights." The right to keep and bear arms is granted in the Second Amendment.

When asked to comment on his use of the English language, the Speaker explained, "I rent these lips on Mondays, and by Friday they are worn out." But not all of what the speaker says is Gibberish. In explaining quality, the Speaker once observed, "It's kind of like buying oats. If you want fresh oats, you got to buy fine-quality oats. But you can buy cheaper oats. The only problem is they've already been through the horse." As the Speaker said, "Think about that for awhile."

Hang it Straight The most novel use of a campaign placard ever devised in Texas came out of the ranch country in South Texas. They use the signs to wean the colts off the mares. All the ranchers do is tie the political signs to the mares' tails and the colts won't go near their mammas.

What About a Poodle? There was a time in Texas when the sure way to win an office was to win the democratic primary. Lyndon Johnson once said that republicans need a passport to enter Texas and he was about half right. A contributor claims he has a relative who is so devoted to the democratic party that he swears he'd vote democratic even if a Saint Bernard was running. That brings up the observation that while the breed is not known, down through the years there have been several dogs elected to office in Texas.

The matter of democrats versus republicans was supposedly put into perspective by Lyndon Johnson. When someone told him a lot of people were voting republican, Johnson replied, "We don't care how they vote as long as we get to count them."

Oldest of All Texas Political Jokes The state representative was awakened by his wife one night who thought she heard an intruder. "Honey," she said excitedly, "I think there is a thief in the house."

The congressman didn't even turn over. He simply replied, "No dear, how many time do I have to tell you. The thieves are in the senate."

Oldest Texas Governor Joke A not so famous Texas governor once went on a hunting trip and, of all things, forgot his gun. No problem; he simply called his secretary with the intention of asking her to ship it to him. Unfortunately, the governor got a poor phone connection and his secretary couldn't understand what he wanted. "You'll have to spell what it is you want," she said.

"GUN," replied the governor, "G as in Jesus, U as in onion, N as in pneumonia. GUN."

The secretary finally figured it out and sent the governor his gun. Once armed, he headed for the hunt. While walking through the brush, he surprised an attractive young lady who was sunbathing in the nude.

"Are you game?" asked the governor. When she said "yes," the governor shot her.

Women's Lib Graffiti seen in Austin, Texas: A woman's place is in the house, not the congress. Someone scribbled in below: A woman's place is in the house, and the senate.

Texas Riddle No. 6: Do you know the difference between a Texas bird dog and a Texas politician? See the last page for the answer.

More Political Graffiti The way the sign was printed it read: Crime does not pay. Underneath someone had scribbled: Neither does farming. And below that someone else wrote: Politics looks promising.

Think About It A Texas politician is like a blind man at a striptease show — he knows what's going on but he wonders what's coming off.

A Favorite Lyndon Johnson Story There was a fellow down in Texas who said to his friend, "Fred, I'm thinking about running for sheriff against Bob Jones. What do ya think of my chances?"

"Well," said Fred, "it depends on which one of you sees the most voters."

"That's the way I got it figured," replied the potential candidate.

"If you see more," continued Fred, "Bob Jones will win. If he sees the most, then you will win sure."

A Texas Hero? Then there was the crafty politician who tried to win votes by claiming one of his relatives had died in the Alamo. What he didn't explain was that the relative died in the Alamo Motel in Big Spring.

An Old Texas Saying If you fool people to get their money, that's fraud; if you fool people to get their vote, that's politics.

That old philosopher Az Tex once observed: The main reason Texas politicians have trouble holding down expenses is that so many expenses vote.

How's That Again? When the famous Ixtock 1 oil spill darkened Texas beaches and everyone was wondering how to clean up the mess, Governor Bill Clements observed, "What we need is a good hurricane."

What'd He Say? John B. Connally decided to run for governor after a young republican named John Tower was elected to the senate and Connally felt Texas was going to hell in a handbasket. During the campaign, Big Bad John appeared on a television broadcast in California and proclaimed "I am running for governor of the United States."

So Much for Computer Graphics Lyndon Johnson once said: A politician who can't feel a situation without having diagrams drawn up for him is no kind of politician.

That old philosopher Az Tex reminds us of a saying he once heard: Politics is the art of promise.

How's That Again? When President Dwight Eisenhower, a native Texan, was asked if government had been lacking in courage and boldness in facing up to a recession, he replied: "Listen, there is no courage or any extra courage that I know of to find the right thing to do. Now, it is not only necessary to do the right thing, but to do it in the right way and the only problem you have is what is the right thing to do and what is the right way to do it. That is the problem. But this economy of ours is not simple that it obeys to the opinion of bias or the pronouncements of any particular individual, even to the President. This is an economy that is made up of 173 million people and it reflects their desires, they're ready to buy, they're ready to spend, it is a thing that is too complex and too big to be affected adversely or advantageously just by a few words or any particular — say, a little this and that, or even a panacea so alleged."

What'd He Say? When Ike was asked about the prospects for peace he replied, "We are going to have peace even if we have to fight for it."

What About His Wedding Day? Former Texas Governor Joseph D. Sayers once said, "A Texas governor has only two happy days; the day he is inaugurated and the day he retires."

That old philosopher Az Tex once observed that the worst politician is one who, after making up his mind, is full of indecision.

Confidence in Who? James "Pa" Ferguson is the only Texas governor, so far, to be impeached. When the courts denied him the right to run again, his wife, Miriam Amanda "Ma" Ferguson entered the race. During one speech in the bitter campaign against a pro-Klan candidate, Ma said, "Hate has been the slogan of the opposition, venom is its password and slander, falsehood, and misrepresentation its platform. A vote for me is a vote of confidence for my husband."

How's that again? Ma Ferguson managed to win the election and become the first woman elected as governor in the United States. During her administration, when the subject of teaching foreign languages in public schools came up, Ma is supposed to have said, "No more of those sinful languages in the public schools. Stop learning our kids dirty rotten French and Spanish. If English was good enough for Jesus Christ, then it's good enough for Texans."

What if Mom Gets Well? Ma Ferguson, well known for the number of convicts she pardoned while serving as Texas governor, once explained her actions. "No dying mother shall plead in vain," Ma said, "for a chance to see again the wayward, unfortunate son before death shall claim her into eternity."

Just Like a Woman Ma Ferguson, during her anti-Ku Klux Klan campaign in 1924, often proclaimed, "Let us take the sheets and put them back on the beds and put the pillow cases back on the pillows where they belong." Also, because she frequently wore a bonnet, Ma would proclaim: "Make a choice; the bonnet or the hood."

How's That Again? Former Governor James Ferguson once said, "When the law gets in the way of practical business, it don't mean anything."

How's That Again? President Dwight David Eisenhower once said, "Things have never been more like the way they are today in history."

How Much *Are* They Worth? W. Lee "Pappy" O'Daniel, a Fort Worth flour salesman, once ran for and won the job of Texas governor. If he lost by one vote, Pappy would have had no right to complain. He couldn't vote because he failed to pay his income tax claiming, "No politician in Texas is worth $1.75." During the campaign, Pappy also proclaimed: "I don't know whether or not I'll get elected, but boy, it sure has been good for the flour business."

Have you heard about the Texas politician who treated the members of his constituency like mushrooms? He kept them in the dark and fed 'em manure.

How's That Again? When Lyndon Johnson was asked about the alertness of his staff he replied, "They aren't walking around with their zippers unbuttoned."

From the "I'd Like to See it Done" Department Sam Rayburn once said, when talking about slowing down the political process: "I like to make running water walk."

A Special Prayer "Lord, here we are again. We sure hope you are too." was the prayer used to open the second special session of the legislature in 1986 which had been called to deal with shortages in the state treasury.

Hope He Ducked The following is attributed to Texas rancher L. C. Brite who was speaking to a women's group that was making noise about a woman running for office: "Women, should you enter politics, who will wash the dishes and burn the bread, sweep the floor and fuss over us carrying in mud, take care of the house, lock the door and lose the key, attend history club and feed us cold biscuits."

Texans Helping Texans When Lyndon Johnson was elected vice president in 1960, the only other Texas VP, John Nance Garner, offered LBJ some friendly advice: "The best way to survive this job is to keep your mouth shut." It was also Garner who claimed being named vice president was the only demotion he ever had. When asked to assess the value of the positions, Garner replied, "The vice presidency isn't worth a bucket of warm spit."

That's Loyalty Once, in explaining that he wasn't overconfident, Lyndon Johnson used the following story: Before a very important election, Lady Bird was in an automobile accident and her car overturned. A reporter asked her, "What was your first thought when you came to?"

She replied, "I thought, I wish I'd voted absentee."

But Did He? During a visit of Prime Minister Harold Wilson in 1964, LBJ claimed Lady Bird gave him some good advice: "This is judgement day," she said, "be sure to use plenty of it."

Lyndon, Where Were You When We Needed You? When Lyndon Johnson was on the ticket with John F. Kennedy in 1959, they faced Richard Nixon. During the campaign LBJ predicted: "Nixon can be beaten. He's like a Spanish horse who runs faster than anyone for the first nine lengths and then turns around and runs backward. He'll do something wrong in the end. He always does." After Kennedy won, Johnson commented, "I just knew in my heart that it was not right for Dick Nixon to ever be president of this country."

He Gets My Vote It has been reported that the shortest campaign speech in Texas history contained just seven words. "Fellow citizens, follow me into yonder saloon."

A Texas Classic A member of the town council called on a local justice of the peace to advise his honor that his court had been abolished.

"But why?" asked the judge.

The councilman responded, "Well, with the bad economy, we had to cut some costs and one court had to be eliminated. We chose yours since it was created last."

"But you can't do that without a hearing," the judge protested

"We've already had the hearing. You lost."

The judge was shocked. "Well, who in this town testified against me?"

The councilman replied, "The head of the local Bar Association for one."

"Let me tell you about the head of the Bar Association," replied the judge. "He's nothing but a shyster lawyer like his daddy and grandaddy before him."

"The mayor also gave testimony against you," added the councilman.

"The mayor," exclaimed the judge, "Why he stole his last election. I happen to know his wife and kids voted three times each."

"There was also the town banker . . ."

"Banker! If that s.o.b. hadn't stole all the money his bank never would a failed."

The councilman, realizing the old judge was getting a little too overheated, finally admitted the whole thing was a joke. "Judge, we didn't eliminate your court. We just wanted to have some fun with you."

The judge slumped back into his chair and breathed a sigh of relief. "Some joke," he said, "making me say those things about three of my dearest friends in the whole world."

Hook 'Em Horns   In Texas, politicians often use the longhorn-type speech. That's one which has two good points, but they are a long way apart with a lot of bull in between.

WARNING!
I do not brake for liberals

From the Texas Bumper Sticker Hall of Fame. Seen in Austin, Texas.

LBJ Pearls of Political Wisdom   Lyndon Baines Johnson, the only real Texan to serve as president of the United States, is responsible for some of the best ever Texas political quotes. Here's a generous sampling:

"A president's hardest task is not to do what is right, but to know what's right."

"Politics is the art of the possible."

"When anyone says he's a country boy, you better put your hand on your wallet."

"What convinces is conviction."

"To hunger for use and to go unused is the worst hunger of all."

"Today our problem is not making miracles — but managing them."

"Controversy, like beauty, is frequently in the eye of the beholder."

"You don't accumulate anything unless you save the small amounts."

"Never sit by a man if there is a lady in the room."

"You never want to give a man a present when he's feeling good."

"Never pass up an opportunity to do an honorable favor for an honest friend."

"Politics is action but it is not civil war. Civil war only comes when truth is forgotten."

"My father used to say if you couldn't walk into a room full of people and tell right away who was for you and who was against you, you had no business in politics."

Winning Friends and Influencing People If you have aspirations toward politics, you will have to be able to win some friends and, on occasion, influence people. While serving in the U.S. Senate, Lyndon Johnson kept a list of the the following rules in his desk where they could be reviewed often:

1. Learn to remember names. Inefficiency at this point may indicate that your interest is not sufficiently outgoing.

2. Be a comfortable person so there is no strain in being with you. Be an old-shoe, old-hat kind of individual.

3. Acquire the quality of being relaxed, easy-going so that things do not ruffle you.

4. Don't be egotistical. Guard against the impression that you know it all.

5. Cultivate the quality of being interesting so people will get something of value from their association with you.

6. Study to get the "scratchy" elements out of your personality, even those of which you may be unconscious.

7. Sincerely attempt to heal, on an honest Christian basis, every misunderstanding you have had or now have. Drain off your grievances.

8. Practice liking people until you learn to do so genuinely.

9. Never miss an opportunity to say a word of congratulation upon anyone's achievement or express sympathy in sorrow or disappointment.

10. Give spiritual strength to people and they will give genuine affection to you.

John Nance "Prickly Pear Jack" Garner once observed correctly, "That government governs best which governs least." If only someone in Washington had been paying attention.

Where's Dorothy? In Texas it is often thought to be a political asset to have rural roots. So much so that many politicians boldly claim they are from the country. Unfortunately, all too many of those politicians are from a county named Oz.

Austin Dilemma Down at the state capital in Austin they have some mighty smart folks and some mighty dumb ones. The problem is nobody can tell 'em apart.

That old philosopher Az Tex once observed: The best politician is the one that can straightforwardly dodge the issues.

Party Loyalty For many years, Texas was known as a democratic state. Back during the Vietnam "unwar," a Marine from Texas was upset because he hadn't had a chance to kill any Viet Cong. He turned to his sarge for advice.

"Well," the sarge replied, "just go up there on that hill and yell 'to hell with Ho Chi Mein' and shoot the first VC that sticks his head out."

The Marine did as he was told but came back from the hill without firing a shot. "What happened," asked the sarge. "Didn't you see any VC?"

"Oh yeah," the Texan replied, "when I yelled, one of them jumped up and yelled back, 'to hell with Richard Nixon.' "

"So, why didn't you shoot him?" asked the sarge.

"I just couldn't kill a democrat."

So That's Why It has been said the state of Texas installed flood lights on the state capitol building so no politician could steal the dome.

A Dobie Tale Sam Houston was a legendary character who was fond of talking and eating. J. Frank Dobie liked to tell about the time Sam was out on the campaign trail and having dinner with some local folks in a small town. Sure enough, once old Sam got started talking he kept it up for hours right through dinner. In fact he got so caught up in his oration that he didn't pay much attention to the food being served. Someone handed Sam a bowl of steaming hot rice pudding, a frontier favorite, just as he was talking about politicians often not using good judgement. He paused, shoveled in a mouthful of the hot pudding and quickly spit it out, instantly remarking "See what I mean. Many a damn fool politician would 'a ate that."

Raise Hell, Not Taxes

From the Texas Bumper Sticker Hall of Fame. Seen on the gas tank of a Harley Davidson motorcycle in Austin.

That old philosopher Az Tex poses an interesting question. If the government can pay farmers not to raise crops, then why can't the farmers pay the government not to raise taxes.

Two Out a Three Ain't Bad Lyndon Johnson, as quoted in a 1956 interview with *Time* magazine said: "You senators and reporters, you better saddle your horses and put on your spurs if you're going to keep up with Johnson on the flag, mother, and corruption."

That old philosopher Az Tex once observed: A politician is one person who doesn't worry about fooling all the people all the time as long as he can fool the majority.

Another Texas Favorite There was the politician who ran for office with high expectations of winning. Unfortunately, the count in the final ballot was 489 to 1 against him. Thoroughly dejected, the man went for a walk downtown. He encountered his local pastor, who was sympathetic. "Jim, I am sorry about the election, but you know you had my vote."

A little while later he encountered the local sheriff who also assured the man, "You know I was the one that voted for you."

As the day progressed, the butcher, the barber, and even a bartender all claimed to have cast the one vote for the man. Finally, in frustration, he went home and announced to his wife, "Pack up, we're leaving. This town is a pack of liars. Everyone claims they voted for me and all the time I was the one that cast that vote."

A city fellow was once running for office and trying to woo the rural vote. He declared, "I was born on a farm; I was raised on a farm; I can plow, plant, milk, hoe, and pick cotton. In fact, there ain't nothin' done on a farm that I can't do."

A voice in the back of the room called out, "Let's see you lay an egg."

Wan'na Rethink That? Back in the early 1950s, Richard Nixon had to face some charges of campaign irregularities which included accepting a small dog from Texas named Checkers. After going on national television to try and clear up the matter, the *Dallas Morning News* of September 24, 1952 reported in an editorial: "This country will have gotten somewhere when it demands Nixon frankness — and Nixon honesty — of every man who asks for its votes."

Good Advice Rarely Followed James A. Elkins, Sr., said, "Remember, you never learn from talkin'. Every fish ever caught on a hook had his mouth open." Sid Richardson later echoed the sentiment, "You ain't learnin' nothing when you're talking."

That old philosopher Az Tex advises: There are two things you should never see made — sausages and laws.

Sam Rayburn is the Texan who served as Speaker of the U.S. House of Representatives longer than any other man in history. During his long and illustrious career, Mr. Sam gave us many pearls of political wisdom. Here's a generous sampling.

"Never commit yourself until you are absolutely sure of your position, and once you give your word, keep it, even if it hurts."

"Age may well bring dry rot as well as wisdom."

"Some men 'ripen' earlier than others and 'burn out' early. Powder will flash but it won't last long."

"When you see a man get stuffy or arrogant because he holds a big job, it means he was not big enough for the job when he got it."

"You cannot lead people by trying to drive them. Persuasion and reason are the only ways to lead them."

"It is easy to be an obstructionist; it's hard to be a constructionist."

"Men are like rocks and when you mix them all up in a barrel, the big ones inevitably reach the top and little ones sieve down to the bottom."

"It isn't how long a man has been in office, but how well he serves."

"A man whose change of position changes his position is lost."

"A politician's got to have publicity to live, but he can damn well get too much of it."

"Anyone can be elected once by accident. Beginning with the second term, it's worth paying attention."

"I know one thing, if a position changes a person that person is not big enough for the position."

"When the work is done, then there is time enough for blowing your horn."

"Any jackass can kick a barn down, but it takes a carpenter to build one."

"Don't count the crop 'till it's in the barn."

It was also Sam Rayburn who once gave his rules that a young person with political aspirations should follow.

He said: Although there is no substitute for hard work, determination, and common sense, here are ten suggestions I have for young people entering politics:

1. Study the history of our country. Learn about the lives of the men who made that history. You will discover that they — Washington, Jefferson, Madison, Jackson, Lincoln and others — were not only statesmen but they were also politicians of the highest type.

2. Study everything you can about political science. Keep up with current events, especially the doings of state governments and the Federal government. Go to political meetings. Attend sessions of your State Legislature and Congress. Talk politics with your friends and neighbors.

3. Start at the bottom. Participate in campus politics, or in city and county politics. When you can, meet the people who run your government at every level. Be willing to do what may seem trivial to you at first. In this way, you'll meet people, find out how they think and feel, and learn what makes them prefer one candidate over another. This is basic political education. You can never have too much of it.

4. Be honest and candid. The people expect our government to be clean, and they expect the men who run it to be clean. No man can last very long in politics without being honest.

5. Always tell the truth. You often have to say "no" to requests in politics. If you tell people the truth and the reasons for your action, you'll retain their respect and, almost invariably, their friendship.

6. Be calm and deliberate in your judgements. Try to get all the facts on both sides of a question. Study those facts thoroughly, then make your decision and stick to it. People lose confidence in a person who is forever making snap judgements and then switching back and forth.

7. Be fair, be just. Be just to everybody under all circumstances. If you are, you will get along with neighbors, friends and members of different political parties.

8. Learn to listen. I have always tried to find time to see anyone who came to my office and wished to see me. A visitor seldom comes who does not bring some information of interest and value — something which helps me to be better informed. All it costs is a little time and the willingness to listen.

9. Don't talk too much. There is a great temptation for public officials and political leaders to talk too much. President Calvin Coolidge once said very wisely, "You never have to explain something you didn't say." If you are sensible in what you say and do not talk too much, people will listen with care and interest to your views.

10. Have faith. It's contagious. If you believe in and trust your fellow man, he in turn instinctively trusts you.

If only every Texas politician had followed the advice of Mr. Sam.

8

Bible Thumpers and Pulpit Pounders

**If you're good and say
your prayers, when you
die you'll go to**

Texas

It comes as no small surprise to many, especially visitors, that Texas — the land of oil fortunes, honky tonks, fast women and faster horses — is known as the buckle of the Bible belt. President George Bush got even more specific when he referred to Lubbock, Texas as the "buckle." Regardless of what visitors might perceive, religion is big in Texas and apparently growing in leaps and bounds. But no matter how popular religion gets, the pulpit will never be immune to Texas humorists. Here's a collection of Texas religious humor to prove that point.

Answered Prayers A Texas preacher was stopped as he was walking to church one Sunday morning by a stranger who asked the man of the cloth to say prayers for Mary Lou. The preacher naturally agreed and did as he was requested. A few days later, the preacher saw the stranger again and asked the man if he wished the praying to continue. "No thanks," the stranger said, "you did your job well. Mary Lou won the fifth race and paid ten to one."

Sounds Reasonable The young Texan joined the Marines during the Vietnam war. Although the youngster had been known to have an occasional fight in a honky tonk back in Texas, he wasn't prepared for the real action of a shooting war. After several days of close hand-to-hand combat, the young man dropped to his knees for a rare prayer. "Lord," he said, "if you'll do your best to watch over me and get me safely back to Texas, I swear right here and now the only thing I'll ever get in trouble for again will be singing too loud in church."

So Long God The little boy knelt down beside his bed for his evening prayer. He thanked God for his blessings, just as he had been taught. Then the boy asked God to please bless his parents, brothers and sisters, pets, relatives, friends, and all the policemen in the world. He ended with a firm amen and started to jump into bed. But he remembered something he had failed to add and knelt down again. "By the way, God," he said, "you probably won't hear from me again. My dad got transferred and we're moving to Texas."

From the T-Shirt Hall of Fame.

Was His Name Neilson? Then there was the old-time Texas preacher who could look over the Sunday morning crowd and predict within a dollar the size of the collection.

That old philosopher Az Tex has observed that a lot of Texans must believe in God, judging from the way they drive. That may explain the sign that once was displayed outside a Dallas church:

LAST CHANCE TO PRAY
BEFORE ENTERING FREEWAY.

Best All-time Texas Preacher Joke In the panhandle, a severe snow storm limited attendance at church one Sunday, so much so that only one old cowboy showed up. When the preacher asked what the cowpoke wanted to do, he replied. "Well, Preacher, if it come a blizzard and I loaded up a pickup and drove out to the pasture to feed the stock, well I believe if only one ol' muley cow showed up, I would feed her.

With that the preacher proceeded to deliver one of his best and lengthiest hell, fire, and brimstone sermons lasting over an hour and a half. When he finished, the preacher asked, "Well, what'd you think of my special sermon?"

"Well, Preacher," the cowboy replied, "If it come a blizzard and I loaded up a pickup and drove out to the pasture to feed the stock, well I believe if only one ol' muley cow showed up I would feed her, but I wouldn't give her the whole load?"

It is widely speculated that all Texans eventually go to heaven because hot air rises.

Good Advice A sign in front of a house of worship in South Texas: "If you are too busy to go to church, you are too busy."

The Ten Commandments are not a multiple choice test.

From the Texas Bumper Sticker Hall of Fame. Seen in Longview, Texas.

Prayers Answered, Almost Lyndon Johnson liked to tell the story of a young man from Texas who sent a letter to God asking for $100 to help out his impoverished family. The letter ended up in the office of the Postmaster General who was so touched, he put a twenty dollar bill in one of his own envelopes and sent it to the youngster.

Two weeks later, another letter from the young man arrived on the postmaster's desk. It read, "Dear God, thanks for all you've done for us but we could sure use another $100 and, please God, don't send it through Washington. Last time they deducted 80%."

Another Johnson favorite was the story about the old farmer who went to church every Sunday, took his seat on the front row, and promptly slept through the sermon.

Finally one Sunday, the preacher became irritated at the weekly event and decided to get even. He said in a soft voice, "All you people who want to go to heaven, please stand up." Everyone except the farmer, who was snoring away on the front row, promptly stood up.

The preacher motioned for everyone to sit down, then said in a loud, booming voice, "Now, everyone who wants to go to hell, please stand up." The farmer woke up in time to hear "stand up" and he leaped to his feet. He then looked around to see the entire congregation, including his wife and kids, still comfortable in their seats. Somewhat embarrassed, the farmer looked up at the preacher and said, "Well, Preacher, I don't rightly know what we're voting on, but it appears you and me is the only two for it."

I'd Like to Know, Too A sign in an Abilene church proclaimed: If you have troubles, come in and tell us about them. If you don't have troubles, come in and tell us how you do it.

A True Test The Texan gave his son a penny and a quarter to take to Sunday school and advised him, "When they pass the collection plate, whichever coin you put in will be a test of how much you love Jesus." The little boy went off to Sunday School and when he returned, his father asked which coin he still had. "Well, dad," the youngster replied,

"I still have the quarter. My Sunday school teacher told us that Jesus sure 'nuff did love a cheerful giver, and I'm tellin' you I was full of cheer when I dropped that penny in the plate."

From the Texas T-Shirt Hall of Fame.

Three small Texans were sitting around the playground bragging about their fathers. "My dad," said the first, "is a heart surgeon and last week he put an artificial heart in an oilman and got $100,000."

"That's nothing," said the second, "my dad is a lawyer and last week he got a famous movie star acquitted in a murder trial and made $250,000."

The third didn't hesitate. "My dad is a Baptist preacher and he has both of your dads beat. Last Sunday, my dad gave such a good sermon that after the collection was taken, it took eight people to carry it to the alter."

The preacher asked the cowboy, "Do you want to go to heaven?"

"No thank you, sir," replied the cowboy.

The preacher was astounded. "Do you mean to say," he continued, "that you do not want to go to heaven when you die?"

"Oh, sure when I die," replied the cowpoke. "I thought you was gettin' up a crew to go now."

That old philosopher Az Tex claims the truest test of faith is to find yourself in church with nothing but a fifty dollar bill in your wallet.

A Simple Request The old-time Texas Ranger captain was in a tough spot. He and his twenty-man regiment were trapped in a buffalo wallow by more than 500 Comanches. As the Indians prepared to attack, the captain turned to the Lord in prayer: "Well God, as you can probably see, me and the boys are in a heap a trouble. I would sure like to request, if you can see your way fit, that you side with us rangers and help us through this engagement." After thinking for a moment, he added, "But Lord, if you can't be on our side, for goodness sake don't be with the Indians. You just stand on one of those hills over yonder and watch the damndest Indian fight you ever saw. Amen."

Diner is Served Surely you've heard about the orphanage in Texas run by a man of the cloth. Whenever meals were served, the preacher always asked the blessing and was certain to touch all the bases. His orations generally took so long that most of the kids were grown and gone before they ever tasted a hot meal.

Sign on a North Texas Church:

> Remember
> Anger is just one letter
> away from danger!

Stained Glass It's been rumored that there's a preacher down Waco way that was so religious that he had stained glass windows installed in his car. Whether or not that is true remains to be seen, but it is definitely not true that that same preacher tried to order stained glass contact lens. It is true however, that his wife had stained glass installed in the bathroom because her husband spent so much time on the throne.

Prayer in Schools Surely you've heard about the small Texan who turned to a friend in school one day and announced, "I don't care if it is unconstitutional, I'm sayin' a prayer before this exam."

A Definition Native Texan Dwight Eisenhower once observed: "An atheist is a man who watches a Notre Dame-SMU football game and doesn't care who wins."

Medicinal Purposes The old country preacher took sick and it appeared his end might be near. His wife cared for him as best she could but the pain was horrible. Finally she asked the doctor if anything could done to ease his pain. "Well" the doctor said, "you could give him brandy each day. That might help."

The preachers wife was aghast, "My husband would never allow spirits to touch his lips no matter how much he hurt."

"In that case," the doctor suggested, "you could put the brandy in some fresh milk so he wouldn't know he was getting spirits."

The wife agreed and for the next several weeks she served her husband a glass of fresh milk laced with a generous portion of brandy. The liquor seemed to help ease the pain, but of course did nothing to halt the disease which ailed him. Finally it appeared the end was near. As the preacher slipped away he called his wife to his side and, with what little strength he had left, whispered, "Whatever you do, don't sell that cow."

Reasonable Question The old Baptist preacher was known for his long-winded sermons. On one Sunday morning his oration was running even longer than usual. Finally a small boy who was growing restless looked up at his mother and whispered in a loud voice, "Mom, if we go ahead and give him the money could we go home?"

That old philosopher Az Tex once observed: The man who thumps his Bible will be less likely to thump his neighbor.

Surely Not It's been said that out in West Texas, a preacher was asked to give a funeral sermon. As he stood beside the open coffin, with the departed's family and friends looking on, the preacher motioned to the casket and said, "We have before us nothing but the empty shell, the nut is gone." The person who told me that claimed it took thirty minutes to revive the dead man's wife.

A church in Abilene once posted a sign proclaiming: All new sermons — no reruns.

Need a Job? The handyman for a North Texas Baptist church retired and the preacher advertised for a replacement. The next morning, a young man arrived and the preacher immediately began asking questions. "First of all," the preacher started, "I'm sure you noticed we have a large lawn. You won't mind mowing it will you?"

The young man answered, "Well, no I suppose I won't."

"And then," the preacher continued, "the pipes in the church are getting old, so are you an experienced plumber?"

"Well, I have had some experience in plumbing," the man answered.

"And of course," the preacher continued, "there will be a lot of carpentry to do as well as some electrical repairs. I think you will be able to find plenty to keep busy."

"Listen preacher," the young man said, "I had no idea there was going to be this much work involved. I think I'll just wait awhile before I get married."

Timely Prayer Lyndon Johnson claimed the most popular preacher in Texas always started his Sundays with a small prayer:

> Lord, fill my mouth
> With worthwhile stuff,
> And nudge me when
> I've said enough.

Sounds About Right Lyndon Johnson once said, "All things are possible when God lets loose a thinker and a doer in this world."

Good Advice Sam Rayburn, the Texan who was speaker of the U.S. House longer than anyone, once passed along this piece of advice: A high standard of living is a desirable thing, but more desirable — and more enduring — is a high standard of life.

Thanks to Dave Brownfield, we learn that there was the old-time Texan who was very religious. Everyone who was a son of a bitch during the week was just an SB on Sunday.

That old philosopher Az Tex has observed: You better do your laughing while you're on this earth. When you die, if you happen to go to hell, you won't want to laugh. If you happen to go heaven, they wouldn't allow laughing.

Church sign seen somewhere in East Texas: We cannot spell success without "U."

Another version seen in West Texas: C H _ _ C H, What's missing?

Best Advice A favorite saying of Mary Crowly, originator of Home Interiors, was, "Be somebody. God doesn't take time to make a nobody."

No Texans Allowed Three men died suddenly and winged their way toward heaven. When the first one approached the pearly gates, he stopped at the checkpoint and St. Peter inquired as to where he was from.

"Ohio, sir," the man said, and he was promptly admitted.

The second man up got the same question to which he replied California. "Come right in my son," St. Peter said with a big ol' grin.

The third man didn't even wait for the question. "I'm from Austin, Texas, sir," he said, "and right proud to be here."

As the Texan stepped forward to enter, St. Peter slammed the pearly gates closed. "Hey, what's the idea?" demanded the confused Texan.

"It's simple," replied St. Peter, "No more Texans allowed. We're tired of you folks from the Lone Star State sitting around heaven complaining about how much better it was back in Texas."

The Sunday school teacher asked the class to draw their favorite picture. When each child had finished, the teacher collected them and showed each one to the class. Most of the kids either drew a picture of what they thought Jesus looked like, or a picture of a church, or something else religious. But little Bubba drew a picture of an old-time cowboy in a saloon. Naturally the teacher was aghast. "Bubba," she demanded, "why did you draw a picture of a man in a place where whiskey is sold?"

"Oh, it's ok, teacher," replied Bubba, "he isn't there to drink."

"Well then, why is he there?"

"He's looking for a gun fight."

Sign on a West Texas Church: Sinners welcome here. No waiting.

Chains that Bind The man from Ohio died and went to heaven. On his first day one of the angels was giving him a guided tour and pointing out all the advantages heaven had over hell. Everywhere the pair went the Ohioan kept seeing people chained up along the side of the roads. Finally his curiosity got the best of him and he asked the angel, "Say, what are all these people doing chained up."

"Oh," the angel replied, "those are Texans. We have to keep 'em chained up to prevent them them from going back to Texas."

A Texas Classic Young Billy Fred swallowed hard when the Sunday school teacher called on him to tell the class where Jesus was born. "Well," he said, "uh . . . was it Athens?"

"No, it wasn't," the teacher replied, "try again."

"OK, uh . . . was it Carthage?" Billy asked meekly.

The teacher shook her head. "Young man, don't you know Jesus was born in Palestine?"

Billy snapped his fingers. "Dang it," he said, "I knew it was some place in East Texas."

Texans believe that God could have built the earth in 4.5 days if He'd used some rawhide. And if He'd used some spit and bailing wire to hold it together, there would be no such thing as earthquakes.

Has it Yet? William H. Jack, an early Texan, wrote a letter home to his mother in 1836. In part, young William said: "There are no churches in Texas, no ministers of the gospel, no religious associations. Mother, I am afraid the way from Texas to heaven has never been blazed out."

A Famous Letter On August 17, 1835, William B. Travis, who would later command the Alamo garrison, wrote one of the most interesting letters of the entire Texas revolutionary period. The letter was addressed to the New York *Christian Advocate and Journal.* Travis wrote:

My Dear Sir; —

I take liberty of addressing you from this distant quarter of the world for the purpose of requesting you to receive my name as a subscriber of your widely circulated Advocate. We are very destitute of religious instructions in this extensive fine country, and the circulation of your paper here will be greatly beneficial, in the absence of the stated preaching of the gospel. Although the exercise of religion in any form is not prohibited here, but is encouraged by the people, yet but few preachers have come among us to dispense the tidings of salvation to upwards of sixty thousand destitute souls. I regret that the Methodist church, with its excellent itinerant system, has hitherto sent the pioneers of the Gospel into almost every destitute portion of the globe, should have neglected so long this interesting country. I wish you would do me and the good cause the favor to publish such remarks as will call the attention of the reverend Bishops, the different Conferences, and the Board of Missions, to the subject of spreading the gospel in Texas. About five educated and talented young preachers would find employment in Texas, and no doubt would produce much good in this benighted land. Texas is composed of the shrewdest and most intelligent population of any new country on earth; therefore, a preacher to do good must be respectable and talented. In sending your heralds in the four corners of the Earth, remember Texas.

9

Home on the Range

**There never has been a horse that can't be rode
or a cowboy that can't be throwed.**

One thing Texas will always be known for are the days of the wild west when cowboys and Indians and buffalo roamed the wide open prairies. Even though the days of the wild west were short lived thanks to the coming of the railroad and barbed wire, that period will live forever in the pages of Texas history. And the rural jokes, though not often in the history books, will also live forever. He are some examples:

Size Counts Some ranches in Texas are so big they are measured by MPG — miles per gate. Of course size doesn't always equate to some people. A West Texas rancher was once entertaining a visitor from New England. After talking fondly of the size of his spread, the rancher concluded, "I can't drive across my place in one day."

The visitor replied, "I know what you mean. We have cars like that in Boston."

A common saying for cowboys traveling through Texas in the old days: The sun has rose and the sun has set, and here we are, in Texas yet.

Perhaps the greatest bumper sticker ever seen in Texas was on a new pickup belonging to a big-time rancher in South Texas. The sticker simply said, "For whom the bulls toil."

A Texas stop sign seen on a ranch.

That old philosopher Az Tex reminds: It takes more to plow a field than turning it over in your mind.

Insufficient Funds Although it's been told many times with only slight variations and always as the absolute gospel truth, here's the oldest of all Texas bumpkin stories: A West Texan was having a hard time making a go of life on the farm. His crops failed, his cattle starved to death, his wife got pregnant, his daughter ran off with a soldier, and his son was lazy. He was about to give up when an oil company approached him about drilling on his property. The farmer decided he didn't have much to lose so he agreed.

Sure enough, as often happened in West Texas, the driller struck oil. When the farmer got his first royalty check, he headed for the bank to cash it. Unfortunately, the teller in the bank handed the check back to the farmer explaining, "We don't have enough money to cash this check."

The farmer was perplexed. "You mean this here bank don't have enough money to cash an $1800.00 check?"

"Sir," the teller replied, "this check is for $180,000."

Back in the old days, it wasn't uncommon for northern "city fellas" to come to Texas to try their hand at ranching. One time this fine Boston gentlemen came to Texas, bought a ranch, and began a new life. After about six weeks, he noticed that many of his cows were disappearing and he suspected his neighbor was rustling them. Now ordinarily that Boston gent would have just charged over there and demanded the return of his cattle but there was a complication. The neighbor was known far and wide as a gunslinger with little patience for Yankees. So rather than confronting the rustler directly, the Boston man decided to send him a note. He wrote: Dear sir, It would be greatly appreciated if you not leave your hot branding irons laying around where my poor cows can lay down on them by accident.

The roundup crew was sitting around the campfire trying to outbrag each other. Billy Fred tried to explain his courage by saying he had encountered a mean bobcat that very afternoon and had defiantly thrown cold water in the cat's face to scare him off. The other cowboys laughed at such a notion until Bubba spoke up in Billy Fred's defense. "Boys," Bubba said, "I 'spect ol' Billy Fred is tellin' us the truth cause I also encountered a bobcat this afternoon and when I stopped to pet him, his whiskers were still wet."

Makes Sense The old farmer was out hoeing cotton when a neighbor stopped by. "Say," asked the friend, "why don't you go to the barn, get your tractor, hook up a cultivator, and plow this field instead of doing it by hand?"

"Because," replied the farmer, "by doing it by hand it is easier to quit when I get tired."

There's an old saying in Texas that you can take the farmer off the farm but you can't take the farm out of the farmer, or something like that. Possible proof of that old saying may have come from the farmer who gave up his land just before he starved to death and moved to the city. He got a job supervising an implement company. About two weeks after he started his new career, a crisis arose over management personnel dating clerical workers. The former farmer was called on to settle the matter and he issued the following directive:

Company policy Number 1.

We do not breed the working stock.

We do not work the breeding stock.

A Texas Classic   The old farmer who had lived most of his life alone finally decided to take a wife. After a short courtship of the town's leading widow, the couple got hitched and headed home in the farmer's mule-drawn wagon. About two miles out of town, the mule strayed off the road to try and eat some grass. The farmer jerked back on the reins and refused to let the mule eat. "That's one," the farmer said, while his new wife looked on in amazement.

After another couple of miles, the couple passed through a small stream and the mule tried to take a drink. Again the farmer pulled up on the reins to prevent it. "That's two," he said.

As the couple neared their honeymoon cottage, the poor old mule spotted some other mules in a nearby pasture and stopped to look. The farmer yelled, "That's three!" He jumped down from the wagon, got a 2 X 4 from behind the seat and proceeded to whack the mule between the eyes, knocking the poor animal senseless. The new wife, who had remained silent, could not hold her tongue any longer, "How dare you treat that poor dumb animal that way," she said. "Why, you might have killed him!"

The farmer looked up at his wife with a sly grin and said, "That's one."

Don't step in our exhaust

From the Texas Bumper Sticker Hall of Fame. This sticker was seen on the back of a horse drawn wagon.

Rural Ingenuity Farmers are a resourceful bunch and have always found ways of getting the most out of anything they did. When slaughtering animals, farmers always strived to use as much of the carcass as possible. Glen Owen, an old-time Texas farmer claimed that when they killed a hog in the old days, they somehow managed to use everything but the squeal.

From the early days, Texas was known for cowboys and big ranches. But then some danged fool invented barbed wire and doomed both the open range and the cowboy's way of life. For many cowpunchers, the transition from ranch to farm was a hard one to accept. The feelings of many a cowboy is explained in the poem, by an unknown author, that was submitted by Jack Glover:

> The boys from Texas are full of wind;
> they'll tell you of their Bowie knife and
> the scrapes they've been in.
> But their powder gets damp,
> and their ridin' hand cramps,
> when they hear the whistle of the cotton gin.

The old cowboy was about to take his first plane ride and he wasn't too sure about it. The stewardess did her best to calm the man down and even told him that chewing gum would help keep his ears from popping. When they landed safely, the stew asked the cowboy how he liked the flight. "You'll have to speak up," he replied, "I can't hear too well with this gum in my ears."

More Rural Ingenuity A farmer down in South Texas once heard that some politicians were going to be traveling through on the campaign trail. The farmer quickly painted a sign and hung it on his front gate. It proclaimed: Goats and votes for sale.

From the Texas T-Shirt Hall of Fame.

Miracle Recovery The old farmer needed some help so he told a friend, "If you'd help me out for a couple of hours, I'll have a ham for you in a day or so."

The friend agreed and gave the farmer a helping hand. Two days, then a week, then two weeks passed and no ham was forthcoming. One day he saw the farmer in town and stopped him to inquire about the missing ham. "Oh, yeah," the farmer said, "I meant to tell you, that old hog up and got well."

Truth in Advertising A few years back, many Texas honky tonks installed mechanical bulls with the hope their patrons would vent hostility trying to ride the bull instead of fighting and breaking up the furniture. But when Billy Bob's Texas, the worlds largest honky tonk, opened in Fort Worth, the management took the bull riding a step farther when they put a real rodeo arena smack dab inside the saloon. To explain the difference between their live bulls and their mechanical counterparts, bumper stickers were printed up proclaiming: Billy Bob's Texas. Where the bulls have real balls not steel balls.

How's That Again? One of the most famous of all Texas ranchers, Abel "Shangai" Pierce, once said: "If I had a cow that'd give gallons of milk, I tell you, I'd never touch a teat. I'd make her stick out her tongue then I'd dip out the milk with a long-handled gourd."

Makes Sense to Me There was a young country boy who was walking to town for the very first time. He happened to come across some railroad tracks and, just as he was about to cross, looked up and saw a train coming straight for him. Since the boy had never seen a train before, he had no idea what it was so he started running down the tracks, doin' his best to stay ahead of the train.

When the young man finally reached town, the railroad agent grabbed the boy and pulled him off the track. "What on earth were you doin', boy?" asked the agent.

"I was tryin to outrun that monster," he said.

"Well why didn't you just get off the track?"

"I knew I was havin' trouble staying ahead of that thing in the open," the boy replied, "and figured I wouldn't have no chance atall in the brush."

Texas Classic My friend Royce Barton likes to tell about the know-it-all named Jones who strolled into the local blacksmith shop one day to inquire if his order for horseshoes was finished. The smith had just finished shaping the last shoe and he set it down to cool. Jones instinctively picked up the hot hunk of metal and subsequently dropped it quicker than a minnow can swim a dipper.

"What's the matter," asked the smith, "too hot for you?"

"Naw," replied Jones, "it just don't take me long to look at a hot horseshoe."

Sign seen on a ranch fence in North Texas near the Red River, and consequently, the Texas-Oklahoma border:

> You are now entering Texas.
> Beware of Bull!

Another Texas Classic An old-time Texas farmer was explaining a new method he had discovered for cutting costs. "One day," he began, "I happened to spill some sawdust into my mule's feed and to my amazement, the stupid critter ate it. Well, that gave me an idea and so I started slipping a little sawdust into the feed every day, increasing the amount each time, and every day, without fail, the mule ate the mixture. I thought I had discovered a sure way to cut my feed bill but it didn't work out."

"What happened?" asked the friend.

"Well about the time I had the mule up to 100% sawdust, he up and died on me."

That Explains It Some Texans have been known to own large ranches and many were never satisfied with even a few hundred thousands acres. W. T. Waggoner was once asked if he intended to buy all the land in Texas. He replied, "No, I only want to buy the land adjoining mine."

From the Texas Bumper Sticker Hall of Fame. Seen on the back of a horse trailer when the only thing you could see was the back of the horse.

Surely you've heard about the old farmer who was such a notorious liar that his wife had to call the hogs for him.

Texas Riddle No. 7: What has four legs, eats hay, sleeps in a stable, and can see equally well from either end? See the last page for the answer.

Cat Lover The visitor from up north stopped at the farm house for directions. He noticed three small openings in the front door and asked what purpose they served. "Oh them's cat holes so the cats can come and go as they please."

"But why three holes?"

"Cause I got three cats."

"Excuse me, but couldn't all three cats use the same hole?" persisted the visitor.

"Spec they could," replied the farmer, "but when I say scat, I mean scat."

Another Cat Lover The old farmer called the vet one day and explained he had a sick cat. The vet suggested he give the animal a pint of castor oil and see if that didn't fix him up. The farmer agreed and did as the vet suggested.

The next day the vet called to inquire, "How's your sick calf?"

"Calf," exclaimed the farmer, "I said cat, not calf."

"Good gawd," the vet said, "you didn't give a cat a whole pint of castor oil did you?"

"I sure did, just like you said," replied the farmer.

"Well how's he doing?" asked the vet.

"Don't rightly know," replied the farmer. "The last time I saw him he was heading out through the south pasture with five other cats. Two were a diggin', two were a coverin' up, and one was scoutin' for more open ground."

Bad Advice Sometimes it's better to have no advice than good advice. A county agent over in Hopkins county saw an old farmer tryin' to dig out some stumps by hand and decided to introduce the farmer to the wonders of dynamite. "A little dynamite under that stump will get it out immediately and save you a passel of diggin'."

The farmer agreed and headed for town and some blasting supplies. A couple of days later, the agent ran into the farmer, who was back in town to buy lumber, and asked how the stump blowin' had gone.

"Well, not too well," replied the farmer. "I got the fuse lighted alright but it went out. Before I could get there to relight it, my prize hog come along and 'et it right up. I took off after him and he ran smack into the barn and scared my old mule half to death. Now you and I both know what a mule does when he's scared — he kicks. Well, sure enough he kicked, caught the hog square in the middle and the jar set off the dynamite. The explosion blew up the barn, broke every window in my house, and mister, let me tell you, I got a mighty sick hog on my hands."

A Lyndon Johnson Favorite Story "You know in Texas, when we go to buy a farm, we don't put too much importance on the man-made disappointments — like a rundown barn or a badly fenced pasture. A good farmer goes out to the fields and sees what's growing. He stoops down and tastes a little bit of the soil. He looks at the stock and the streams and the spring. If these are ample or can be made so by the sweat of his brow, the farmer knows the place holds a future. I grew up on that land. Some of it was mighty poor and rocky — but some of it was good. I learned not to be afraid of disappointments — of the weeds and rocks — but to value the good soil and the hard, constructive work."

A Texas Classic The New York yuppie decided to chuck the good life and see what it would have been like to be a pioneer. He moved to Texas and bought a farm. He naturally went into town for supplies and ended up at the implement company where the salesman did his best to sell the man a new tractor.

"No, no," replied the New Yorker, "I want to live like the pioneers. I want to plow my fields from behind a mule."

"I ain't got no mules," replied the salesman.

"Ok, I'll keep looking," replied the New Yorker as he started to walk away.

Now that old salesman realized that he was dealing with a greenhorn of the first order and decided to have some fun. "Say, fella," the salesman said, "there ain't no full-grown mules in these parts but I do have a nice mule egg that's about to hatch." He motioned to a large watermelon one of his customers had brought in. "All you'd have to do is take it home, keep it warm, and a week or so you'd have a fine baby mule that you could raise the way you want."

"Well how much is it?" asked the New Yorker.

"Because I like you, it's only $100," replied the salesman.

The New Yorker bought the "mule egg" and headed home in his wagon. About half way there, he hit a dip in the road and the jar caused the watermelon to bounce out and it landed on the side of the road with a splat. As the farmer raced back to check on his egg, a jackrabbit took off running and that New Yorker gave chase. But the rabbit was just too fast and it got away.

A month or so later, that New York farmer was back in town and he encountered the implement salesman in the cafe. "Say," asked the salesman, "how'd that mule egg work out for you?"

The New Yorker told his story and the salesman, fighting back a laugh, replied, "it's a shame that baby mule got away."

"Oh, it's ok," replied the New Yorker, "he would have been too fast to plow behind anyway."

Rest of the Story That New Yorker finally learned that he had been tricked and resolved such would never again happen to him. When he later went to town looking for a bird dog to go hunting with, he refused to pay for the dog unless the owner would pitch it into the air to prove it could fly.

From the Texas Bumper Sticker Hall of Fame. This sticker was made popular by Nocona Boots.

The Adventures of Billy Fred and Bubba Billy Fred and Bubba were out working the range when they spotted a bobcat up a tree and decided to have some fun. Bubba said, "I'll shinny up that tree and chase him down and you put him in a sack."

With that Bubba took off his spurs and climbed up the tree. When he reached the right limb, he started shaking and sure enough the cat came tumbling down. Billy Fred grabbed the varmint by the back of the neck and tried to put him into a sack. The damndest commotion you ever heard broke out with scratching and dust flying in all directions. Bubba called down, "What's the matter, you need help catching one little ol' bobcat?"

"Hell no," replied Billy Fred, "I need help turnin' him a loose."

More Adventures of Billy Fred and Bubba Billy Fred and Bubba were camped out in the Big Bend and getting ready for bed when they heard a bear growl. They decided it wouldn't be wise to go to sleep and leave a bear on the prowl so it was concluded that someone had to shoot the varmint. Now Bubba wanted to do it, sure enough, but Billy Fred wouldn't have none of it. "After the way you messed up that bobcat episode, I 'spect I'll handle this here bear all right. You get some sleep."

Billy Fred grabbed his rifle and disappeared into the night. He hadn't gone twenty-five yards when perhaps the largest bear ever seen in Texas suddenly stood up and charged. In the sudden excitement, Billy dropped his rifle so he started running back to camp yelling at the top of his lungs "Shoot the bear, shoot the bear!"

Bubba heard the commotion, grabbed his gun, and killed the bear with a single shot. "Well," he said, "at least I never ran away from that bobcat when he come out of the tree."

"I didn't run away from that bear either," Billy answered, "I was just bringing him back to camp for you."

Yet Another Billy Fred and Bubba Adventure Cowboys out of Big Spring, Texas were up north somewhere on vacation. They went into a local tavern for a peaceful glass of beer but one of the regular patrons of the establishment just wouldn't leave them alone. The stranger made fun of the way the Texans dressed and how they talked. But being peace loving, Bubba and Billy Fred just sat there trying to mind their own business. But then the big-mouthed stranger made a serious mistake. "As I understand it," he said, "all the women in Texas are either as fat as a hog, ugly as a horned toad, or have the morals of a $2.00 hooker."

Well, it so happened that Billy Fred and Bubba were both married to Texas women, which meant the loud mouth had insulted both their women, something no Texan will ever sit still for. The two good old boys from Texas flipped a coin to see who would have the pleasure of taking the stranger out back and whipping some sense into him. Bubba won the flip and immediately invited the stranger to settle the matter man to man. The loud mouth agreed and both men headed for the back door with most of the people in the bar, including Billy Fred, following close behind expecting to see a good fight.

Once outside in the alley, the stranger suddenly produced a switch blade knife and said he was going to split Bubba open like a ripe watermelon. He never got a chance. As soon as Bubba saw the knife, he drew a pistol that was hidden in one of his boots and shot the loud mouth right between the eyes, killing him instantly. As Bubba turned to go back inside and finish his beer, he said to Billy Fred, "Ain't that just like a damn Yankee to bring a knife to a gunfight."

Don't call him a Cowboy, 'till you've seen him ride.

From the Texas Bumper Sticker Hall of Fame. Undoubtedly inspired by the Conway Twitty song on the same subject. Incidentally, you might call Conway Twitty half a Texan. His name was derived from two towns, Conway, Arkansas and Twitty, Texas.

Classic City Slicker Story Seems this city fella approached the old farmer and asked simply, "Have you lived here all your life?"

"Not yet," replied the farmer.

Another City Slicker Classic The second oldest city slicker joke: The "city fellow" hadn't the faintest idea where he was so when he overtook a lad, he brought the car to a halt and asked, "How far is it to Dallas?"

"Dunno," said the boy.

"Which way is Dallas then?"

"Dunno."

"Well, where does this road go to?"

"Dunno."

Exasperated, the traveler said, "You don't know much do you?"

"Naw," answered the boy, "but I ain't lost."

Yet Another City Slicker Classic That same city slicker was driving along a country road when he happened onto an accident where a load of manure had spilled out of a wagon. A young man was busy shoveling manure and hurling it in all directions and the city man decided to offer some advice.

"Young man," he said, "perhaps I can help. I am an efficiency expert from Dallas. Now instead of hurling that manure all over the place, why don't you simply take your time and shovel it back into the wagon. That way you won't have to handle it twice."

"That ain't the way my paw raised me."

"Well, perhaps I could explain to your father, where is he?" asked the city fella.

"Under this load of manure."

Indian Brave? The agent was driving an old Indian back to the reservation during a freezing norther. Despite having on several pair of long johns and an overcoat, the agent was about to freeze to death. The Indian, on the other hand was almost naked but appeared to be doing fine.

"How do you do it?" asked the agent, "I'm about to freeze to death."

"Is your face cold?" asked the Indian.

"No but everything else is."

"Me all face," replied the Indian.

Good Advice Never ride a horse named Tornado, Whiplash, Backbreaker, or Widowmaker.

Have you hugged your Horse today?

Fight Smog, Ride a Horse

Two classics from the Texas Bumper Sticker Hall of Fame.

Insurance Woes A friend in the insurance business swears this is the strangest claim they ever had. An old rancher filed a claim and offered the following explanation:

"I was having trouble with coyotes out on my place and I tried everything to get rid of 'em but nothing worked. Well sir, one day I was out in the pasture blowing up some stumps with dynamite. Sure enough, one blast uncovered a mangy old coyote who was hiding in a burrow. Now, I knew I had to kill the critter but I didn't have no gun with me, only dynamite. So, while that varmint was still dazed, I caught him and strapped two sticks of dynamite to his back. I figured that was one ol' coyote that wouldn't be botherin' me no more. An' I was right, too. The only thing is, about the time I put a match to the dynamite fuse, the coyote recovered and run off. He was just passin' under my new pickup when the dynamite exploded."

That old philosopher Az Tex wonders why it is you can dodge a longhorn bull or wild horse, but you can't avoid a housefly.

A Lot of Cattle A Texan and a fella from Nebraska were having a friendly discussion about ranching and, try as he did, the Texan was having trouble outbraggin' the Nebraska fella. The Texan finally bragged about having 3000 head of cattle, probably the most in Texas.

"That ain't nuthin," replied the man from Nebraska, "we got a lot a ranchers with more cattle than that."

"Oh," replied the Texan. "I forgot to mention. That's how many I have in the deep freeze."

And Cantaloupes Too Some places in Texas, the soil is so fertile, they can't plant watermelons because they grow so fast they rub off the rind.

A Texas Dozen Down in the Rio Grande Valley, they grow grapefruits so large that it only takes nine of them to make a dozen.

Branded for Life There have been some humorous Texas stories about cattle branding handed down through the years. One of the most famous was about the man who got killed while trying to steal a cow. The jury found the rancher innocent but the dead man's brother got revenge when he killed the rancher. The brother was subsequently hung which meant one cow caused three deaths. Someone took up his branding iron and burned the word murderer into the cow's side and turned her loose. For years ranchers would report seeing the cow but no one ever caught it. Some say the ghost of that cow still roams the Texas prairie.

The most famous brand story, however, had to do with the art of changing the brands on stolen cattle, which was a common practice among rustlers. One rancher, who used the brand IC on his cattle, began to miss some of his herd. He rode over to a neighbor's ranch and found the neighbor was using the brand ICU. The rancher was convinced some of his cattle had had a U added and he was determined to get even. Late that night he rustled what he felt were his own cattle and added 2 to the brand for ICU2.

About two weeks later, the rancher again counted his herd and was amazed that still more were missing. He immediately rode over to his neighbor and was horrified to see several thousand head of cattle all branded OICU2.

Yankee Farmer We wouldn't say Yankees are stupid, but there was the case of the northern fella who went into farming and got his tractor stuck in reverse. He unplowed three acres.

Really Rural Some places in Texas are so far back in the woods that it takes awhile for modern life to reach them. I have a friend who swears he lived so far out in the country that when he was growing up, they didn't get the Saturday night radio broadcast of the Grand Ole Opry until Tuesday morning.

He also swears that his mother and father were sittin' out on the porch one day when one of those new ultra-light airplanes came flying overhead. Never having seen anything like it before, the farmer quickly got his gun and started shooting at the plane. On the third shot, he scored a hit and black smoke started streaming from the plane's small engine. In the next instant the pilot fell off and plummeted to the ground. When it was over, the farmers wife asked, "What was that thing pa?"

"Don't rightly know," replied my friend's father, "but I sure made it drop that fella it was carryin'."

Another City Slicker Classic The city slicker was visiting a dude ranch and wanted to take his first ride ever on a real horse. His ignorance showed through when he said to the ranch foreman, "Since I've never ridden before, how about giving me a horse that has never been ridden so we can start even."

The amused foreman complied and as the dude was about to mount, he asked for instructions on how to ride. "It's easy," said the foreman, "just put one leg on each side and keep your mind in the middle."

Well, that dude got his ride all right, and when he finally got back to the stable after several hours, he was heard to comment, "I didn't think anything filled with hay could be that hard." He spent the rest of his vacation standing up playing bridge with the ladies.

Serious About Guns Texans, especially rural Texans, seem to have a natural attraction for firearms and most do not appreciate anyone trying to mess with their right to keep and bear arms. To illustrate that, here are three members of the Texas Bumper Sticker Hall of Fame:

You can have my gun when you pry it out of my cold, dead fingers

REGISTER COMMUNISTS!
NOT TEXAS FIREARMS

Sure, you can have my gun, but it'll be after the fight.

What's in a Name? The farmer was in town for a little Saturday buying and the storekeeper asked, "Well, what did you name your new son?"

"Can't name him till one o' the dogs dies," the man replied; "cause the dogs got all the good names."

Related Story Tom Tomlinson swears this is a true story. Tom says that when his father was born, he was the tenth child and his parents had run out of good names (perhaps the dogs had 'em). As a compromise, Tom's dad had to settle for initials only — L. G. That worked fine until it came time for L. G. to go school where everyone was required to have real first and middle names. When asked for his name, he said L. G.

"No," replied the school teacher, "I need you entire first and middle name."

Undaunted, he replied "It's L only and G only."

That satisfied the teacher and she completed her form. For years Tom's dad was known as Lonly Gonly.

Sign in a Texas Dairy: You can't beat our milk, but you can whip our cream.

Texans not only have the most horses, they also have the best trained horses. Perhaps the best of the bunch was a horse that belonged to an old time cowboy out in West Texas. One day that cowboy was riding along not really paying attention to where he was going and he rode off a thousand foot cliff in Palo Duro canyon. Naturally, everyone who saw the incident assumed both horse and rider had plunged to their death. You can imagine their surprise when they rushed to the rim of the canyon and looked down to see horse and rider leisurely trotting off as if nothing had happened. When the cowboy finally made his way back to the top of the canyon, his buddies were quick to ask how he had managed to survive.

"Hell, boys," he replied, "there weren't nuthin' to it. When we went off that cliff I knew we were in trouble. But then I remembered I had trained that horse to always do what I said, so when we got about five feet from the bottom, I just yelled whoa real loud and my horse stopped right there. From that point, it was an easy jump to the bottom."

Sound Logic An old-time farmer was sitting on the porch of his cabin deep in the woods of East Texas when a city slicker stranger approached.

"What do you raise?" asked the stranger, trying to make conversation. "Hogs," replied the farmer.

"What else?" continued the stranger.

"That's all — just hogs."

"Why don't you raise something besides hogs?" the tourist persisted.

"Cause hogs don't need no plowin'," the Texan replied.

Rest of the Story It seems everyone tried to poke their nose into that old farmer's business. The county agent stopped by one day and tried to convince the farmer to try a new brand of hog feed.

"This new feed," explained the agent, "will help your hogs grow twice as fast so you can get them to market quicker."

"Not interested," replied the farmer.

"Why not?" persisted the agent.

"Because," answered the farmer, "time ain't nothing to a hog."

About two weeks later, the agent decided to try again to convince the farmer to try the new feed. As he pulled up to the farm, he noticed the house was on fire but the old farmer was sitting under a tree. The agent jumped out of his car and yelled, "Man don't you realize your house in on fire?"

"Yep," the farmer replied without any show of emotion.

"Well aren't you going to do something about it?" asked the agent.

"Yep," replied the farmer, "ever since the fire broke out, I been sittin' right here praying for rain."

From the Texas Bumper Sticker Hall of Fame. The Texas version of a national favorite.

Postscript A friend from town was visiting that farmer and was intrigued by the odd behavior of his hogs. The animals were out in the woods running wildly from one tree to another.

"What in the world is ailing your hogs?" asked the friend.

The farmer spit out some tobacco juice and replied, "A few weeks back I come down with a severe case of laryngitis and plumb lost my voice. Since I couldn't call the hogs, I had to beat on the fence with a stick whenever it was feedin' time. After a couple a days they figured out what that sound meant and would come a runnin."

The friend still didn't understand. "But you have your voice back now so what are the hogs doing?"

"The woodpeckers are about to drive them crazy."

How's That Again? "What is the best way to keep milk from souring?" a stranger asked the old farmer. He replied, "Leave it in the cow."

Believe it or Not Crops are usually measured by things like bushels per acre. However, when mother nature doesn't cooperate, crops are often not too plentiful. One year in West Texas, the corn crop was so bad it was measured in individual servings per acre. A friend who was visiting the area that year swears he ate three acres of corn at one sitting.

New Math The school teacher asked Bobby Jack, "If you had twelve sheep and one jumped over the fence, how many would you have left?
"None," answered Bobby.
"Well you certainly don't know subtraction," replied the teacher.
"Maybe not," answered Bobby, "but I know sheep."

More New Math When a New York visitor asked the Texan how many cows he had, the Texan replied "exactly 612."
"How do you know?"
"I count the legs and divide by four."

Wanna Buy a Horse? Former Governor Jim Ferguson was a horse trader of some renown and reputation. He was also, according to some, a politician who would pardon criminals for a price. One day a father came to Jim with an urgent plea for clemency for his son. While they talked, Farmer Jim took great pains to point out an old flea-bitten nag he had for sale.
"You wouldn't want to buy a horse would you?" Jim asked.
"No, I'm here about my son" the man replied.
"You sure you don't want to but a horse?" Jim persisted.
"Yes, I'm sure. I'm here to try and get my son out of prison. What would I do with a horse?"
"Well," Jim said, "your son could ride him home from prison."

Texas Riddle No. 8: What do a woman and a cow patty have in common? See the last page for the answer.

A Sign of the Times Did you hear about the Texas rancher who sold his ranch on account of poor health. He was sick and tired of losing money.

Six Flags it Ain't! Northwest of Houston, a farmer has hit on an idea to make milking cows a paying proposition. He has a large sign out front proclaiming: Milk a cow here. The idea is that when the transplanted city slickers from Houston come out for the weekend to enjoy the scenery they can also experience a real part of rural Texas by actually milking a real cow — for a price. While the visitors are entertained, the farmer gets his milk and some spending money to boot.
Not far away, another farmer expanded the idea. For a fee, anyone who has never experienced life on the farm can spend the weekend

plowing, hoeing cotton, slopping hogs, and the like. Although there is no confirmation, it's been rumored that while the city folk are working on the farm, the farmer and his wife head for Houston to go shopping at the Galleria.

A Rancher's Philosophy: Famous Texas rancher W. T. Waggoner once said,

"A man who doesn't admire a good steer, a good horse, and a pretty woman, well, something is wrong with that man's head." It was also Waggoner who uttered one of the most famous Texas quotes of all time. While digging for water on his 6666 ranch, Waggoner struck oil. "Damn it," he said, "cattle can't drink that stuff." He was right but he ended up making enough money from oil that he could have imported water if he wanted to.

Lost in Translation   The call came into the news desk that some pigs had been stolen from a local farmer. Since it was a slow news day the editor dispatched a reporter to write the story. When the reporter returned, he handed the story to a typesetter who was fresh from New York and not well versed in rural life.

When the story ran the next day, the reporter was amazed to see that 3016 baby pigs were reported lost. He immediately challenged the typesetter, who defended himself with "that's what you reported."

"No it's not," replied the reporter. "I reported '3 sows and 16 baby pigs' were stolen."

A Native Texan   The King Ranch, one of the world's largest, developed the only true American breed of cattle, the Santa Gertrudis. The ranch once ran an advertisement in the *Western Livestock Journal* that showed a picture of a splendid Santa Gertrudis bull above the headline "There's money in his genes."

Sign on a South Texas Ranch   Drive safely, the life you save might either be next Sunday's dinner or next Thanksgiving's feast, or next year's rump roast.

From the *Texas Bumper Sticker Hall of Fame*. Seen on the bumper of a pickup driven by Glen Owen, a sure 'nuff tobacco chewer.

World's Worst Cowboy Joke Did you hear about the honest cowboy? He named his horse Hi Ho Stainless.

World's Oldest Rattlesnake Joke Perhaps because of their ominous appearance and dangerous bite, the Texas rattlesnake has found its way into the state's wit. Here is perhaps the oldest, and possibly the best, rattler joke:

Billy Fred and Bubba were out hunting when Bubba had to go to the bathroom. Since there were no facilities available, he had to squat down behind a small bush. Unfortunately he didn't notice a coiled rattler nearby and no sooner had he dropped his pants than he received a painful bite squarely on the rump.

Bubba screamed in pain and called for Billy Fred to get a doctor. Billy ran back to the pickup truck and drove to the nearest phone to call for medical help. After hearing the situation, the doctor said someone would have to immediately lance the wound and suck out the poison. "If you don't do it," the doc said, "your friend will die."

When Billy Fred got back to camp, Bubba was getting anxious. "What'd the doctor say?" he asked.

"Billy Fred," Bubba replied. "I'm afraid the doc said you're gonna die."

Poachers Beware The rancher in South Texas was having a serious problem with poachers killing his game. He tried everything including no trespassing signs, hiring private guards, and adding more locks to his gate. He was about to give up and move to the city when he decided to try one more thing. He had several signs erected proclaiming: Rattlesnake Sanctuary. The poachers haven't been seen since.

Sign on a South Texas Ranch Attention Hunters: Please don't shoot anything that isn't moving. It's probably either my hired hand or my son.

The absolute best sign ever seen on a Texas ranch:

Watch your step,
the chips are down.

Fast Learner Farmers are often portrayed as little more than country bumpkins but it is not always so. There was a farmer over in East Texas who went down to buy a new pickup. He found one he liked and the price seemed right until the dealer added in all the extras. Disgruntled, the farmer bought the truck and went home vowing to one day get even. He got his chance sometime later when the car dealer, who also happened to be a weekend rancher, approached the farmer to buy a cow. After the car dealer picked out the one he wanted, the farmer presented the following bill:

Basic cow	$100
Two-tone finish	45
Two-barrel stomach	75
Real cowhide upholstery	125
Produce storage bin	60
Four spigots ($10 each)	40
Dual horns	15
Automatic fly swatter	35
Field fertilizing device	45
Total price for cow	$540

Wanna Buy a Ranch? Despite all the hardships, the secret dream of every Texan is to one day own his ranch in the country. If the bug bites you, you might want to heed the advice of Dick Yaws, former Farm and Ranch director for WBAP radio in Fort Worth, whose own small ranch was called Oleo because it was a cheap spread. Here are Dick's minimum requirements for ranching:

1. A wide-brimmed hat, one pair of tight pants, and $20 boots from a discount house.

2. At least two head of livestock, preferably cattle — one male, one female.

3. A new air-conditioned pickup with automatic transmission, power steering and trailer hitch.

4. A gun rack for the rear window of the pickup, big enough to hold a walking stick and rope.

5. Two dogs to ride in the bed of the pickup.

6. A $40 horse and $300 saddle.

7. A gooseneck trailer, small enough to park in front of a cafe.

8. A little place to keep the cows, on land too poor to grow crops.

9. A spool of barbed wire, three cedar posts, and a bale of prairie hay to haul around in the truck all day.

10. Credit at the bank.

11. Credit at the food store.

12. Credit from your father-in-law.

13. A good neighbor to feed the dogs and cattle whenever the owner is out in Colorado fishing or hunting.

14. A pair of silver spurs to wear to barbecues.

15. A rubber cushion to sit on for hours at the auction ring every Thursday.

16. A second-hand car for going out to feed the cows when your son-in-law borrows the pickup.

17. A good pocket knife, suitable for whittling to pass the time at the auction ring.

18. A good wife who won't get upset when you walk across the living room carpet with manure on your boots.

19. A good wife who will believe you when you come in at 11 p.m., saying "I've been fixing the fence."

20. A good wife with a good full-time job at the courthouse.

10

Chicken Chronicles

**The lowly hen is immortal
because her son never sets.**

Although she has never gotten the publicity of the longhorn steer, the armadillo, or even the rattlesnake, the lowly chicken has been important to Texas from the days of the republic.

Chicken references have certainly found their way into the language of Texas. Poor handwriting is called "chicken scratching." Someone who is really excited is "nervous as a chicken trying to pass a square egg." Anyone walking funny is "walking around like a chicken with an egg broken inside." A person might be "busy as a chicken trying to drink water out of a pie pan." An angry individual is usually "mad as a wet hen." And of course, you should take care not to "put all your eggs in one basket" but if you do, be sure to watch that basket.

The most common language usage involving the lowly chicken is when someone acting crazy is said to be "running around like a chicken with his head cut off." The phrase originated by the wild motion the body of a chicken often goes through immediately after being beheaded in preparation for an invitation to Sunday dinner. Although the phrase has been used for generations, it is wrong. Chickens are females; roosters are males. But somehow "running around like a rooster with his head cut off" just doesn't sound right. Here's a small collection of chicken humor.

Chicken farmers are an inventive bunch. When a certain milk company advertised its milk as coming from contented cows, a Texas chicken farmer followed with the slogan "eggs from contented chickens." But the best example of ingenuity came when Ford Motor Company was still building cars in the Lone Star State. Each vehicle carried a sticker in the back window proclaiming "Made in Texas by Texans." A poultry farmer not wishing to be outdone by the automobile giant, advertised that his eggs were "Laid in Texas by Texhens." That same farmer also decided to sell some baby chickens to help meet expenses. He hung a sign on his front gate: Cheepers by the dozen.

Lucky Rooster Of course, it is a fact that many chickens ultimately end up on the dinner table either at home or in a restaurant. There has always been some competition among the restaurants to offer the best possible

135

chicken to their customers. One cafe in northwest Texas was so sure of the quality of his meals that he boldly advertised "If there is a better piece of chicken the rooster is gettin' it."

How's That Again? Have you ever stopped to consider that the rooster is one of few animals in the world that has his pecker on his head. In *Once a Cowboy,* Walt Garrison explained the situation of a rookie in an NFL training camp. He said, "You're on the bottom of a very rigid pecking order and you find out right away you're the chicken with the little pecker."

What, No Pullets? The most famous chicken ranch of all was once located near the small town of La Grange, in central Texas. The "Chicken Ranch" was a bit different than most, however, because they were selling something other than pullets. It was, perhaps, the most famous whorehouse in the world. The place got its name back during the depression when farm boys couldn't come up with three dollars so they would trade chickens for services rendered. It's been said that during the really bad times, many a farm boy went hungry on Sunday because he was at the "ranch" on Saturday night.

When they were, as we say in Texas, fixing to close down the Chicken Ranch, Larry King, one of the state's native sons, came home to cover the event for Playboy Magazine. The story he wrote, *The Best Little Whorehouse in Texas,* ultimately became a popular broadway play and ended up a movie staring Dolly Parton and Burt Reynolds. Thanks to the Chicken Ranch, ol' Larry King probably got more out of one whorehouse than any man in history.

For some reason, joke writers have always sort of associated the chicken with roads. A popular joke was once: Why did the chicken cross the road? The simple answer was: To get to the other side.

The next generation of the joke was: Why did the chicken cross the road? To prove to an armadillo that it could be done.

The latest version is: Why *didn't* the chicken cross the road? She was tired of all the jokes.

The best version is: Why did the chicken go only halfway across the road? See Texas Riddle No. 9 on the answer page.

It's a Chicken Life Chickens don't always have life easy. The folks in East Texas claim the soil is so fertile that when a farmer throws shelled corn to the chickens, they have to catch it on the fly or eat it off the stalk.

Another farmer claims the advent of daylight savings time has almost wrecked the chicken industry in Texas. He says the extra hours of light are causing the chickens to almost work themselves to death trying to lay two eggs a day.

The worst case of chicken abuse came from a Texas Aggie. Seems the Aggie decided to raise chickens so he bought two dozen baby chicks and promptly planted them head first in the ground. Naturally, they died.

Undaunted, the Aggie purchased two dozen more chicks, but this time he planted them feet down. They still died.

Instead of buying more chicks, the Aggie decided to turn to his alma mater for help. He sent the animal husbandry department at Texas A&M a long letter detailing all that he had done and asking why the chicks had died. The A&M officials replied, "Unable to make determination with information provided. Send soil samples."

Chickens beware! With all the talk about beef perhaps being harmful, many people have begun eating more poultry. A good friend Hal Ragan decided to side with the cattlemen and launched the "Help The Beef Business, Run Over A Chicken" campaign.

That old philosopher Az Tex has observed that chickens are the laziest animals on the farm because all they do is lay around.

Chickens Beware You may not know it but hogs will, on occasion, eat a chicken, guts, feathers, beak and all. Years ago, a newspaper writer was asked about a cure for a chicken-eating hog. His advice was to shoot a rabbit and throw it into the hog pen. According to the newsman, a hog is so stupid he couldn't tell a chicken from a rabbit and would eat the thing. Unfortunately for the hog, rabbit fur is a lot harder to digest than chicken feathers, and the the old hog will suffer mightily, making him much less eager to try a rabbit or a chicken ever again.

The poor chicken has also found its way into politics. The first time republican Bill Clements ran for governor was during the Carter administration. His highly favored opponent was democrat John Hill. Clements explained his campaign strategy with: "I'm going to hang

Jimmy Carter around John Hill's neck like a dead chicken." He did, and it worked.

How's that Dear? Although it's not too common, eggs do serve other purposes than food. A husband was cleaning out the family closet recently and found a box with three eggs and $112. When asked, his wife broke down and admitted that whenever she had an affair she would place an egg in the box. The husband was understandably upset but then he decided that since they had been married thirty years three eggs would mean an average of one indiscretion every ten years and that wasn't too terrible. However, he was perplexed. "But what about the money?" the husband asked.

"Oh," the wife explained, "everytime I got a dozen eggs, I sold 'em for a dollar."

Truth in Advertising Then there was the restaurant which advertised: "Wingless, backless, neckless fried chicken."

It's Time To Cull Your Flock

Get rid of your non-layers and replace them with young chicks.

An actual advertisement that appeared in Texas papers during the 1930s.

Ode to the Hen Although much has been published about the chicken, none did a better job than former Governor Pat Neff. His article, entitled simply "The Hen," was published while he was president of Baylor University. The governor wrote:

The hen, hatched and raised in the lowly environment of the barnyard, has scratched her way to fame and fortune. Though she lives and labors in humble surroundings, her cackle — like the voice of freedom — is heard around the world. Hers is a universal language. It is understood wherever the tongues of men fashion the symbols of speech. Her beauty is unhonored in the realms of art but she is known wherever the dinner bell is heard or the banquet board is spread.

Hers is not the elfin grace of the swan. Hers is not the sweet song of the canary. Hers is not the colorful glory of the peacock. Hers is not the arrogant pride of the eagle. And yet all these feathered favorites combined do not rank as high in the affairs and the affections of men as does the placid, the diligent, and the unpretentious hen.

"Pay as you go," is the hen's policy. She is self-sustaining. Not long ago, a carload of hens was shipped from Texas to New York and they laid enough eggs on the trip to pay for the freight.

This is an age of substitution. We substitute cotton for silk, oleomargarine for butter, and jazz for music. But there is no satisfactory substitute for the vitamin contents and mineral compounds of an egg. The hen has less than a teaspoonful of brains and she boasts of no college degree; yet she is the most expert alchemist of the ages. She mixes, in her simple laboratory, her elements of calcium, magnesium, iron, sodium, potassium, chlorine, sulphur, and phosphorized fats — mixes them into rich and well-balanced nutrients in a sanitary and protective shell. She defies the world to make a substitute.

The home is the hub of humanity. On its stability, civilization depends. The hen is a home-maker. She supplies the table, fills the wardrobe, and lifts the mortgage. The farm wife of the henless home has no bank account. The hen is the only servant that can just "lay" around the barnyard and still make money.

The hen, feathered aristocrat of the barnyard, the only billion-dollar bird beneath American skies, should be our national bird. No longer should the selfish, haughty, arrogant eagle, which never earns an honest dollar, adorn the nation's coin. Contrary to the American spirit, the eagle makes war on smaller birds and steals its daily food from creatures too weak to protect their own. All you can say in favor of the eagle is that it flies above the clouds and builds its nest high on the mountain crag. Its meat, its eggs, and its offspring are worthless in both the homes and the marts of men.

The image of the honest, patient, efficient hen who, by picking up the scattered grain and turning it into gold, has made her business one of the biggest industries beneath the American flag — hers is the image that should go upon our coin. She graces alike the paltry meal of the plebeian and the epicurean board of the plutocrat.

She cackles but she does not crow. Her daughters are everywhere; her sons never set. Hats off to the hen!

11

Aggie Jokes

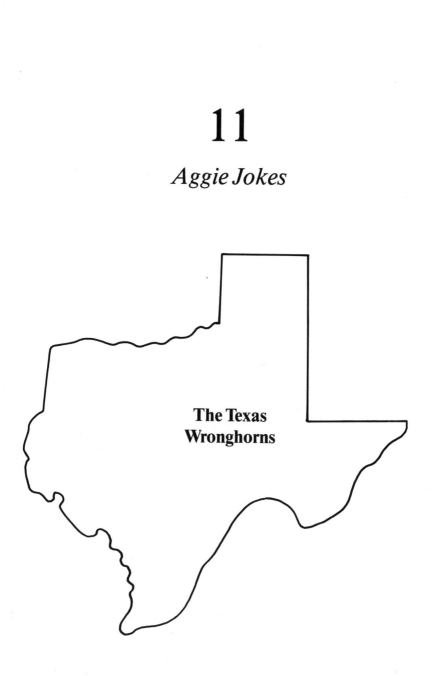

**The Texas
Wronghorns**

Almost every society has its favorite target for puns. The habit probably started with the Romans making Christian jokes. Nowadays, Southerners have Yankee jokes, Northerners tell Polish jokes, and city folk tell country hick jokes. In Texas, we tell Aggie jokes. No one knows how the practice got started but it has gone on for years, probably since A&M students first started calling themselves Aggies. One of the oddities of Aggie jokes is that you often hear the very best ones from A&M students and graduates. With absolutely no disrespect to Aggies, here is a collection of some of their best jokes.

Oldest Aggie Joke? Perhaps the oldest of all Aggie jokes is the one about the cadet who marched in the band. His parents came to watch him perform during a halftime of a football game, and when their son missed a step, the mother proclaimed, "Oh, look they're all out of step except our son."

Texas Riddle No. 10: Do you know how many Aggies it takes to milk a cow? If you don't, turn to the last page for the answer.

It's a Girl! You may have heard that Shamu, the killer whale at Sea World in San Antonio, had a baby girl. It is not true that Tamu was the father of the baby. TAMU stands for Texas A&M University.

The Death of an Aggie
An Aggie wasn't feeling well so he went to the doctor, who was a fellow Aggie, for a checkup. The Aggie doctor spent a lot of time examining the patient but was unable to make an exact diagnosis. Finally he confronted the patient and said he had good news and bad news.

"Let me have the bad news first," said the Aggie patient.

"Well," said the Aggie doc, "after all the tests I still don't know exactly what ails you."

"And the good news?" asked the Aggie.

"I'll know a lot more," replied the doc, "after the autopsy."

That poor ol' Aggie was naturally scared so he went to another doctor for a second opinion and was told that, incredibly, he had just hours to live. Since there wasn't time to do anything worthwhile with what remained of his life, the Aggie decided to spend his last few hours where he was most happy — in bed with his wife. He hurried home, told his wife the sad news, and invited her to go to bed. She agreed but told him not to get any ideas about having sex.

"Why not," cried the Aggie, "I have only hours to live."

"Exactly," said Mrs Aggie, "and I need my rest because I have a funeral to attend tomorrow."

Well sure enough, that poor ol' Aggie did die as expected. His well-rested wife went to order the headstone but was perplexed as to what to have written on it. "Well," said the monument maker, "Rest in Peace is our most popular phrase." Mrs Aggie agreed and was told it would be ready in about a week.

The lady buried her husband and then, a couple of days later, attended the reading of the will. She was shocked to learn that her supposed faithful husband had left half of everything to his mistress-secretary and the other half to his alma mater, Texas A&M.

Infuriated, Mrs. Aggie went immediately to the gravestone maker to have some changes made. She was too late; the stone was finished.

"Can't you make any changes?" she asked.

"No ma'am, it's carved in stone."

"Well, can you add a line?" she asked.

"Yes, one line, that's all," the man said.

Mrs. Aggie thought for a moment. "Very well," she said, "below 'rest in peace', I'd like you to carve 'till I get there.'"

While the wife was busy planning her revenge, the Aggie winged his way to heaven. When he arrived, Saint Peter felt sorry for him because of the way his wife had treated him on his last day and offered to have him reincarnated immediately as anything he wanted. The Aggie thought for a moment and decided. "I want to be a stud in Dallas," he said. In the next instant he was transformed into a 2 x 4.

Texas Riddle No. 11: What do you call a smart person on the A&M campus? Answer on the last page.

Poor Baby The Aggie and his wife became the parents of a new baby boy and a few days later took the little future Aggie home. After three days, however, the parents noticed a strange odor and quickly took the baby back to the doctor. After examining the little Aggie, the doctor asked, "Have you been changing the diapers on this baby?"

"Not yet," replied the Aggie. "I read the instructions on the box and they said the diapers were good to forty pounds."

The Aggie Dilemma Did you hear about the Aggie who heard that most accidents happen within twenty-five miles of home so he moved. About the time that Aggie got settled in his new house, he heard that four out of five accidents happen in the home so he moved again, this time into an apartment.

Texas Riddle No. 12: Do you know how to tell when an Aggie has been working on a computer? If you don't, the answer is on the last page.

The Aggie Wing of the Texas Bumper Sticker Hall of Fame

My son and my money
go to Texas A&M

Shown exactly as it appears on most cars.

A&M TEXAS
WRONGHORNS

My son is a Texas A&M Honer Stewdent!

Undergraduate Version.

My son is a Texas A&M
Honor Graduete!

Graduate Version.

HONK IF I'M AN AGGIE

The All-Time Best Aggie Bumper Sticker.

Will Rogers never met a TEXAS AGGIE

Produce Haulers Two Aggies decided to go into the produce hauling business. They bought a truck and headed for the valley. They purchased a truckload of watermelons at $1.50 each and headed for farmer's market in Dallas to sell them. Unfortunately, in Dallas the merchants were selling watermelons for $1.00 each so the Aggies followed suit and quickly sold out.

They went back to the valley and picked up another load of $1.50 watermelons and headed back to Dallas. When they arrived, they found dealers selling watermelons for $.75 so they sold theirs at that price.

On their way back to the valley, they got to talking about how great is was to be self-employed without any time clocks or bosses to worry about. "The only thing is," said one Aggie, "I wish we were making more money."

"I told you," replied the second Aggie, "that we should have bought a bigger truck."

Those same Aggies continued in the produce hauling business and continued losing money. After several more watermelon trips they decided to try to carry some special freight to make extra money. A man in the valley had a monkey he didn't want and offered to pay the Aggies $100 to take it to the Dallas zoo. They agreed and left with the monkey. When the Aggies came back in a week, they still had the monkey with them.

"I thought you were gonna take him to the zoo," said the merchant.

"We did," one of the Aggies replied, "and it was so much fun, this week we're gonna take him to a Ranger game."

AGGIE DUCK CALL

Reprinted courtesy of Gigem Press, P.O. Box 64445, Dallas, Texas 75206.

An Aggie Classic After several losing seasons, the A&M football coach decided to seek heavenly intervention. Accordingly, before the first game of the new season, the Aggie coach asked for God's help in winning the game. Sure enough, the Aggies won a decided victory.

Bolstered by such events, the coach again turned to heaven for help before the next game and the Aggies won their second in a row. The coach followed the same procedure for each succeeding game and the team always won. But then it was time for the annual turkey day game against arch rival Texas. Just before the kickoff, the Aggie coach turned to God for some real help, "Father," he said, "You've really been good to us so far and if you can see your way clear, we need your help one more time. All we ask is a little assistance in beating the Longhorns. Amen." Shortly after the prayer the Aggies went out and got soundly whipped 55 to 0.

Following the game, when all the stands were empty, all the players gone, and only the cleanup crew remained, the Aggie coach walked to the center of the field, got down on his knees, and spoke to heaven. "Father, why did you fail us in our hour of biggest need?" he asked.

At that point some ominous clouds gathered in the heavens; lighting danced in the sky and thunder rolled across the stadium. In the next moment, the Aggie coach heard a deep, resonate voice, proclaim from beyond the clouds, "Hook 'em Horns."

I am an
~~Agie~~
~~Aggee~~
~~Aggi~~
I go to A&M

From the Texas T-Shirt Hall of Fame.

A graduate of the A&M Engineering department applied for a job as an air traffic controller. To be sure he didn't use drugs, he had to take a urine test; but after studying all night, he managed to pass it. When he went to take his physical, the doctor told him to strip to the waist so he took off his pants. The doctor set him straight and the Aggie passed the physical. Next in the employment process was an oral examination. The first question on the test was, "If you saw on your radar screen that two planes at the same altitude where flying straight toward each other, what would you do?"

"I'd call my brother," answered the Aggie confidently.

"Call your brother?" asked the examiner, "What for?"

"Cause he ain't never seen no plane crash."

Beat the Hell Out of 'Em Many Aggie students hang signs outside their rooms encouraging their team to beat the hell out of their next opponent. A year or so ago, when no game was scheduled, the sign read "Beat the hell out of Open Date."

Aggie History Maker Then there was the Aggie who was taking a correspondence course during the summer. One day he decided to go fishing instead of completing his lesson, so he sent in an empty envelope. It's the only time in history anyone ever cut class in a correspondence course.

Finally! At a recent Longhorn versus Aggie football game, someone fired a gun in the stands. The Longhorns, thinking time had expired, left the field but the Aggies continued to play on. After running only seven more plays they finally scored.

Surely you've heard about the Aggie who came across the newly painted park bench with the sign "Wet Paint" so he did.

Surely Not! Then there was the recent Aggie football player who graduated but still couldn't read. He spent $50 to get into a warehouse. The next day, that Aggie bragged to his friends that he had spent the night in the best little warehouse in Texas.

He Was No Fool An Aggie took a summer job with a construction company in Houston and was assigned to work on the sixty-fifth floor of a new skyscraper going up. On his first day, the Aggie almost stumbled and fell off but his supervisor caught him just in time.

"Boy that was a close call," said the Aggie.

"Naw it wasn't," said the supervisor, "even if you had fallen off you would have been OK."

"What do you mean? asked the Aggie.

"Well, you see there is a big updraft here in downtown Houston," the supervisor said. "If you had fallen off, when you got to about the 20th floor, the updraft would have caught you and brought you right back up."

The Aggie was dumbfounded. "No way I'm gonna believe that one."

"Here, I'll prove it," the super said and off he jumped. Sure enough, he fell to about the 20th floor and then just flew back up with the updraft. The Aggie was amazed.

"See I told you. Why don't you try it so you won't be scared?"

Although hesitant, the Aggie agreed. He jumped off the building, promptly fell 65 floors, and ended up in a major splat on the ground below. When it was over, another worker came up to the supervisor and asked why he was so mean.

"Because I just hate Aggies," Superman replied.

What If They All Went? Surely you've heard about the Texas A&M student who moved to Oklahoma and raised the IQ level of both states.

A&M students don't seem to make good paratroopers. One time an instructor told the Aggie trainee to jump out of the plane, yell Geronimo, and pull the rip cord. The Aggie jumped all right but he didn't get too far. As the instructor was about to launch another jumper, the first Aggie appeared outside the door of the plane wildly flapping his wings like a giant bird. "What'd you say was the name of that Indian?" he asked.

When that Aggie was about to make his second jump, the instructor decided to make things a little easier on him. "All you have to do," he said to the trainee, "is count a thousand and one, a thousand and two, and so on till you reach a thousand and ten. Then pull the rip cord. Do you understand?" The Aggie shook his head affirmatively and jumped into the wild blue yonder.

Everyone watched with anxious anticipation for the Aggie parachute to open but it never did. The Aggie crashed down through a stand of trees, landing on a hay stack, and bounced into a mud puddle. When the rescue team got to him, they found him bruised but alive. When asked what happened, all the Aggie could say was 687, 688, 689 . . .

Finally, the instructor was so exasperated, he decided to jump with the Aggie to show him how it's done. As the two cleared the airplane, the instructor asked if he was ready to pull the cord. Not yet.

The pair continued to free fall for another thousand feet and the instructor asked the same question. Again the Aggie said no. After another ten thousand feet of free fall, the instructor insisted it was time to pull the cord. "Not yet," replied the Aggie.

"What are you waiting for?" demanded the instructor.

"With all the trouble I've had learning how to parachute, I think I'll just wait until I'm close enough to the ground and then jump down."

Postscript Riddle What do the Aggies call a paratrooper whose chute doesn't open? Answer on back page.

Texas Riddle No. 13: How do you drive an Aggie crazy? Answer on back page.

Poor Aggies When the telephone company began its 1 + long distance system, the lives of most Aggies were ruined because the phones do not have a + sign.

A Great Catch One of the greatest Aggie receivers of all time got a job as a fireman during one summer vacation. On his first call, a young mother and her six-week-old baby were trapped on the top floor with no way down. The fire chief urged the woman to drop the baby to safety.

"I won't do it, you might drop him."

"No we won't, one the best pass catchers with Texas A&M is here and he will surely catch your baby."

Reluctantly, the woman finally agreed, closed her eyes, and dropped the infant. Sure enough, the Aggie made a spectacular catch. The crowd, which had gathered, immediately began to cheer and the Aggie responded by doing a little dance and spiking the baby.

Wrong Book An Aggie who wanted to learn more about being close to women went to the library and spent the day reading How to Hug. He didn't learn much, however, since it was the seventh volume in a set of encyclopedias.

Surely Not Some Aggies actually think diarrhea is hereditary because it runs in your shorts.

What'd He Say? Three soldiers of fortune were scheduled to die before a firing squad in South America. Realizing they were in a tight spot, the three decided their only chance was to try and create some diversion to allow them to escape.

When the day came, the first man was marched out and stood before a wall. At the moment of truth, he yelled "tornado" and while all the startled soldiers were scrambling for cover, he jumped over the wall and disappeared. When order was restored, the second man was brought out. He yelled "earthquake" at the moment of truth and escaped in the confusion. Finally it was time for the last man, a graduate of Texas A&M, to face the rifles. When the general ordered Ready, Aim . . . the Aggie interrupted and yelled "Fire!"

How an Aggie holds his likker.
Reprinted courtesy of Gigem Press, P.O. Box 64445, Dallas, Texas 75206.

Sock it To 'Em Then there was the Aggie who went down to Padre Island for spring break. He really wanted to impress the girls so he asked the advice of a Longhorn friend. "Do like I do," said the Horn, "wad up a sock and stuff it in your bathing suit." The Aggie decided to give it a try and went off looking for a sock.

Two hours later the Longhorn met the Aggie on the beach. "How's it going?" asked the Longhorn

"No good," answered the Aggie, "Your sock trick isn't working. I ain't picked up a single girl. Got any more ideas?"

"Well," answered the UT student, "you might try putting the sock in front."

Helpful Aggie In the days before lethal injections, the state of Texas used an electric chair for executions. One particular day three inmates where scheduled to die. When the first was all strapped in, the warden ordered the switch thrown but nothing happened. "Well," said the warden, "by law we have to let him go. Bring on the second man."

Again, when the order to throw the switch was given, nothing happened so the man was released. Finally a frustrated warden ordered the third man, an electrical engineer from Texas A&M, strapped in. "This may be your lucky day," said the warden, "we can't seem to get this chair to work." The Aggie looked down and grinned at the warden. "There's your problem warden, you forgot to plug in the chair."

Texas A&M University
English 101

Bad Grammar don't help no Aggie's image. Follow the following rules when preparing Term Themes:

1. Corect spelling is essential.

2. Don't use no double negative.

3. Make each pronoun agree with their antecedent.

4. Join clauses good, like a conjunction should.

5. About them sentence fragments.

6. When dangling, watch your participles.

7. Verbs has to agree with their subjects.

8. Just between you and i, case is important too.

9. Don't write run-on sentences they are hard to read.

10. Don't use commas, which aren't necessary.

11. Try not to over split infinitives.

12. Its important to use your apostrophe's correctly.

13. Proofread your theme to see if any words out.

Reprinted courtesy of Gigem Press, P.O. Box 64445, Dallas, Texas 75206.

Blame it on Detroit Did you hear about the Aggie who locked his keys in the car and it took him three days to get his date out. That same Aggie was riding in the back of a pickup truck that suddenly went out of control and off a bridge into a lake. The poor Aggie drowned because he couldn't get out of the pickup — the tailgate wouldn't open.

Makes Sense Then there was the Aggie graduate who enlisted in the army. When he was assigned to the cavalry, the Aggie protested and asked for another outfit. "I don't understand," said the sergeant, "everyone else is anxious to get into the cavalry. What's your objection?"

"Well, sir," the aggie replied, "sooner or later we are going to have another war. When that happens, I might be in a company that was forced to retreat. If that happened, I wouldn't want to be slowed down draggin' no damn horse with me."

Did you hear about the Aggie who thought Drano was a laxative? What about the Aggie who wanted to become a ham operator so he hooked up an antenna to his pig? If you haven't heard of these two Aggies, its probably because they died tragically when they went to a drive-in movie and froze to death waiting to see "Closed for Winter."

Aggies Can Read! Then there was the Aggie graduate who submitted his application to the Dallas police department. No, he didn't want to be a policeman. He had seen a headline in a Dallas paper which proclaimed: Man Wanted For Rape. That same Aggie once caused quite a stir in his anatomy class when he asked what part of a woman was her yet.

"I've never heard of such a thing," replied the teacher.

"Well, it must be true," said the Aggie, "cause I saw a headline in the Dallas paper. It read: Woman shot, bullet in her yet."

An Aggie Tragedy Texas A&M once had an ice hockey team for a short time. The entire team drowned during spring practice.

Another Aggie Tragedy After trying ice hockey, the Aggies turned to water polo. Unfortunately the team had to disband when all the horses drowned.

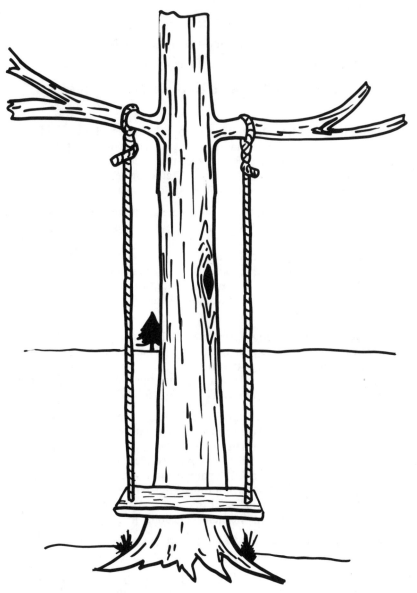

How the Aggie engineer designed a tree swing.

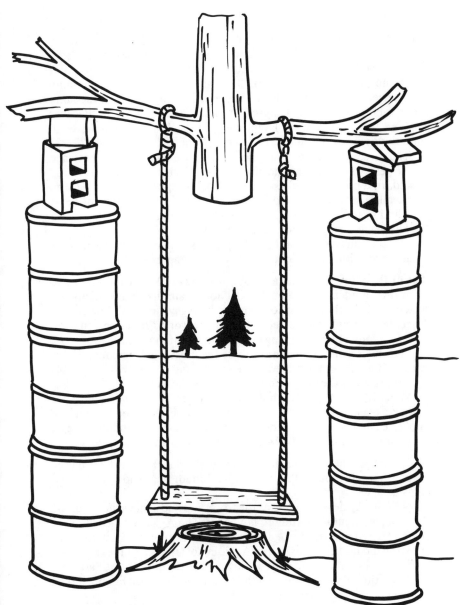

How the Aggie engineers built it.

The Aggie and the Genie Three college students, one each from Texas, Texas A&M, and Texas Tech, were on a summer cruise when the ship suddenly sank and they were forced to swim to a nearby island. After several months of lonely isolation, the Aggie stumbled onto a magic lamp and hurried to show the others. The Texas student examined the lamp with a rubbing motion that caused a mystical genie to appear. "Because you have freed me from the lamp," the genie said, "I am empowered to grant three wishes and three wishes only. What is your command?"

The three students held a quick conference and decided that each should get a wish. The Longhorn went first. "I wish I was back in Texas," he said. In a poof of magic smoke, he was transported back to Austin. The Red Raider was next, and he also wished to be back in the Lone Star State and in an instant he was sent on his way to Lubbock.

The genie turned to the Aggie. "And what is your wish?"

"Gee, I don't know," said the Aggie, "it's gonna be awful lonesome around here without my friends. I wish they'd never left."

Rest of the Story That same Aggie, who was exiled by the other two when they suddenly came back, later found another magic lamp and decided to keep the wishes for himself. "For my first wish," he said to the genie, "I want to be the richest man in the world." In the next instant, the Aggie found himself sitting on a mountain of money.

"For my second wish, I want to be the most handsome man in the world." The genie smiled, blew some smoke, and instantly — incredibly — the Aggie was the most handsome man in the world.

"Finally," the Aggie said holding his crotch, "I want to be built like my horse back in Texas." The genie smiled and disappeared in a puff of smoke, leaving behind the richest, most handsome, well-endowed Aggie in the world, still stranded all alone on a desert island.

Aggie Science The Aggie scientist set out to run an experiment. He placed a frog on a table and yelled "jump" real loud. Sure enough, the frog jumped.

Next the Aggie cut off one of the frog's legs and again yelled "jump." The frog again jumped, though not as far. The Aggie proceeded to cut off the second and third frog leg and yell for it to jump. Each time the little frog did his best. Finally, the Aggie cut off the last of the frog's legs and yelled "jump" as loud as he could but the frog didn't move. Satisfied, the Aggie turned in his report on the experiment in which he concluded: If you cut off a frog's legs, he goes deaf.

Next Experiment Bolstered by his success, that Aggie scientist embarked on another experiment. Although it cost a small fortune, that Aggie has finally proven that the last thing to go through a fly's mind when he hits a car's windshield is his butt.

Rest of the Story Based on his two successes, that Texas A&M scientist has applied for a research grant to determine how a thermos bottle knows to keep coffee hot and iced tea cold. Knowing the government, he'll probably get the grant.

From the Texas T-Shirt Hall of Fame. Shown as actually printed on the shirts so when asked, the Aggie can look down and read where he goes to school.

Aggie Answers When students apply for admission to Texas A&M, they are required to complete a questionnaire. The following are answers supplied by one prospective Aggie:

Age: — Atomic
Place of birth: — hospital
SEX: F M — My radio only gets AM
Church preference: — red brick
Nationality: — Democrat
Have you ever been convicted of a felony: — No, I only date girls
S.A.T. score: — I've never even been to San Antonio, Texas, much
    less scored there
Have you received any financial aids: — No, I wore condoms
Have you applied for a Scholarship: — No, I get seasick.
Will you be living off campus: — No, I live off my parents
Marital status: — eligible
Course of study: — S.I.*
Preferred degree: — 75

*When asked to explain this entry, the prospective Aggie replied Civil Engineering.

An Aggie Mother Writing to Her Son:

Dear Son,

Just a few lines to let you know that I'm still alive. I am writing this letter slowly because I know you can't read fast. You won't know the house when you come home — we've moved. There was a washing machine in the new house when we moved in, but it isn't working too good. Last week I put in four shirts, pulled the chain, and ain't seen the shirts since.

About your father, he has a lovely new job. He has five hundred people under him — he's cutting grass at the local cemetery. His boss sent home a note that said if the last three installments on your grandmother wasn't paid in a week, up she comes. You might prepare yourself to have a roommate when you come home to visit.

As for family news, I got my appendix out and a dishwasher put in. Your sister Jewel got herself engaged to that fellow she's been going out with. He gave her a beautiful ring with only two stones missing. The wedding will be in two weeks which is about right since the baby is due in three weeks. As soon as the baby comes and I find out if it's a boy or girl I will let you know whether you are an aunt or uncle.

Your uncle Dick was drowned last week in a vat of moonshine whisky. Two men dived in to save him but he fought them off bravely. We had the body cremated and it took the undertaker three days to put out the fire. We were going to put his ashes on the mantle but the urn tumped over and Jewel vacuumed Uncle Dick up. I suppose he'll be just as happy in the city dump.

The weather here has been OK. It only rained twice last week, once for three days and once for four. Monday the wind blew so hard the chickens had to lay the same eggs twice. Your father and I were going to sit outside and enjoy the warm weather but the wind blew the sunshine completely off the porch. Also, thanks to the wind, we learned our new neighbors keep hogs. You father says we can count on having fresh ham every time the neighbor goes on vacation.

I must close now since it is almost sundown and I haven't learned to write in the dark.

Your loving mother

P.S. I was going to send you $10 but I had already sealed the envelope.

Her Son's Reply:

Dear Ma,

It was nice to read from you again after all this time. I am glad you got a new house. Please send me the address so I will know where to go when I come home for a visit. Come to think of it, I'll need the address before I can mail this letter so send it right away.

I'm glad you got a new washing machine. Maybe the four shirts will eventually show up. You should see what we have down here at A&M. They're sort of like white tubs that hang on the wall. There's a whole bunch of tiny holes in the bottom and when you pull the handle a little water fall starts. It's the best way on earth to wash your hair but so far I seem to be the only that has discovered what they are supposed to be used for.

Things are going real well in school, especially remedial reading. I am up to about twenty-five a minute so the next time you send me a letter you can write as fast as you want and I'll be able to read it fine. Also, please tell Pa to send me on down my rifle. Next semester I'm taking triggernometry and I want to practice up.

Also, tell Pa congratulations on the new job. As for grandma, if she has to come up you might want to send her on down here to Texas A&M. She would fit right in with the other girls. Also, since she's only been dead two years I'd say she has a fair shot at being elected homecoming queen.

I was sure sorry to hear about Uncle Dick drowning in that vat of whiskey. But I bet he was so happy when he died that it took the undertaker three days to get the smile off his face. I wish I'd known you was gonna have him cremated. You could have saved some money by sending him down here and I'd a put Uncle Dick on our annual bond fire.

When Jewel has her baby, please let me know if I'm an aunt or an uncle so I'll know what color to paint my room.

With love,

Your Aggie sun

P.S. The winds blows strong here too. Just last night it blew John Wayne off his horse at the drive-in movie.

The Aggie heard about the new fad to take milk baths in an effort to stay young and he decided to give it a try. After he got all settled in the tub, the attendant asked if he wanted the milk pasteurized. The Aggie replied, "No just up to my neck, I'll splash some on my face."

Boring Texas A&M University Press has announced they are coming out with a married man's version of Playboy Magazine. It's the same magazine except that the centerfold never changes.

How's That Again? The Aggie went to an optometrist and said he needed glasses because he couldn't tell heads from tails.

"Oh, are you a gambler?" asked the optometrist.

"No, I'm a dentist," the Aggie replied.

Reasonable Question The Aggie got on a plane and sat down next to a lady nursing a baby. "That sure looks like a healthy baby," the Aggie said.

"He should be," the lady replied, "I only feed him milk and orange juice."

"Oh really," said the Aggie, "which one is orange juice?"

Did you hear about the laziest Aggie in the world? He was 10 years old before he got a birthmark. That same Aggie grew up to become a noted researcher and spent most of his life trying to find a cure for cabin fever.

Aggies Measure Up Two Aggies were holding up a flag pole and doing their best to measure it without much success. A stranger happened along and suggested that if they laid the pole down on the ground it would be easier to measure. "That won't work," said one of the Aggies. "We want to know how tall it is, not how long."

Best Aggie Joke? In his great book *The Best of Texas,* Kirk Dooley claimed the following was the best Aggie joke:

Two Aggies decided to try ice fishing. They gathered up their gear and marched off onto the ice. Just as they started chopping a hole, they heard a voice proclaim, "There's no fish there."

The Aggies shrugged, moved a few feet, and started chopping again. They stopped when the voice repeated, "There's no fish there."

Puzzled, the Aggies called out, "Who's that talking?"

The voice replied, "This is the manager of the Galleria."

Another Opinion Kirk may be correct. However, everyone seems to have his or her favorite Aggie joke. Here's my nomination for the *second* best Aggie joke of all time:

A man went into a saloon and asked the bartender if he'd like to hear the world's best Aggie joke. The bartender wasn't amused.

"Before you start tellin' Aggie jokes in this bar," he said, "you better know that the deputy sheriff sitting over in the corner is a former Aggie. You should also know that the 300-pound professional wrestler sitting with the sheriff is an Aggie."

The bartender motioned to another corner and continued, "You see those two big old boys over there, they were linebackers for the Aggie football team a few years back." The bartender then produced a shotgun and laid it on the bar. He concluded, "As for me, I graduated from A&M ten years ago. Now, mister, do you still want to tell an Aggie joke?"

The man thought about it for a moment then said, "No, I think I'll pass. I don't have time to explain it five times."

Absolute Best Aggie Joke of All Time And finally, here's my nomination for best Aggie joke ever told:

Three college students, one from Texas University, one from Texas Tech, and one from Texas A&M, saved up their money and went to Seoul for the Olympics. The only problem was it took all their cash just to get to the games and there was nothing left over for event tickets. In desperation, they decided to try to fake being contestants so they could get in.

The Longhorn found an old broomstick and quickly whittled a point on one end. He marched up to the gate and proclaimed, "U.S. javelin team." The guards admitted him without challenge.

The Red Raider dug an old frisbee out of his bag, cleaned it off, and marched up to the gate. "U.S. discus team," he said, and the guards allowed him to pass.

The Aggie was perplexed because he couldn't think of anything. Finally he got a list of events and, as he read, an idea flashed in his mind. He dashed out of the stadium and found a hardware store. In no time he was back carrying a roll of wire over his shoulder. He marched up to the guards and proudly proclaimed, "U.S. fencing team."

12

Aggies Revenge

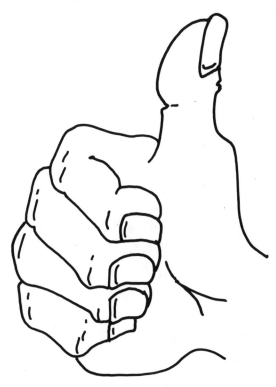

Gig 'Em Aggies

In fairness to the Texas Aggies, there have been plenty of jokes about other schools. Here are some of the better ones.

Do you know what you call an Aggie who has been out of school for a year? Boss.

Southern Methodist Did you hear about the SMU coed who suddenly withdrew from school. When the dean asked why the sudden departure, the coed replied, "My reason will soon be apparent — and so will I."

An Austin condominium.

Oklahoma Have you heard that next year's broadcasts of Sooner football are going to be carried on the police band. They want to make sure that any player being arrested won't miss the action.

Baylor Surely you've heard about the Baylor students who went door to door soliciting funds for the relief of Venetian blinds.

North Texas Did you hear about the student at North Texas University who was out on a date. When his girl asked if he wanted to see where she was operated on for appendicitis, he replied, "No thanks, I can't stand hospitals."

That same North Texas girl had a date with another young man a couple of nights later and she asked him the same question. When he replied "Hell yes" to seeing where she was operated on, she took him to the veterinarian's office.

Rice The Rice graduate went up north on vacation and stopped by to see the original copy of the Declaration of Independence. He was amazed to see that the entire document was written in italics.

Tennessee Did you hear about the University of Tennessee football player who thought that a bar stool was something Davy Crockett stepped in?

Texas Christian Did you hear about the new organization on the TCU campus? It's called D. A. M., Mothers against dyslexia.

Baylor Did you hear about the Baylor students who wanted to ban violence on television? They picketed the Waco TV stations to stop broadcasting weather reports.

Southern Methodist Some students at SMU were once asked their opinion about the greatest contribution chemistry had made to the world. The single most popular answer was "Blondes."

Oklahoma State The OSU senior was asked to explain the difference between electricity and lightning. He replied, "You don't have to pay for lighting."

Texas Christian Then there was the TCU coed who went storming into the registrar's office one day. She waved a copy of her entrance application and demanded to know why she had been given an F in sex when she hadn't even taken the course.

Louisiana State The LSU anatomy class was asked if anyone could identify the different genders. One student boldly raised his hand and answered, "There are the male sex, the female sex, and insects."

Texas Tech Know how you can tell when someone graduated from Texas Tech? They have TT on their ring.

Southern Methodist Know how you can spot an SMU student? He has yellow stains on the front of his designer tennis shoes.

Sam Houston State Two students from Sam Houston were out on a date and having dinner at a fine restaurant. When the waiter asked if they would have red or white wine with dinner, the Sam Houston student replied, "It don't matter, we're both color blind."

University of Texas Ever wonder what happens to all the students who can't make it at Texas A&M? They have their middle two fingers cut off and are shipped to Austin.

Houston Did you hear about the University of Houston student who got arrested? When he was given one call, he dialed information.

University of Arkansas Paper Recycler.

University of Texas El Paso The UTEP graduate got a job in Houston and went out to celebrate his first night in the big city. He wanted to eat at a good restaurant, so he picked the one with the largest ad in the yellow pages and went into a phone booth to call for reservations. Two hours later he was still in that phone booth trying to decide how to dial "Established 1901."

Rice Did you hear about the scientist down at Rice planning to send a rocket to the sun? When an Aggie pointed out that the rocket would melt, the Rice student replied, "Stupid Aggie, we're gonna launch it at night."

Texas Christian Did you know the police department in Fort Worth has stopped putting 911 emergency stickers on their squad cars? TCU students kept stealing them thinking they were Porches.

Oklahoma Texas A&M economists have finally found a way to solve the prison overcrowding in Texas — ship half the convicts to Oklahoma on football scholarships.

Baylor Did you hear about the Baylor student who got arrested for decent exposure? He wore clothes to a nudist colony.

Arkansas Surely you know the definition of "gross ignorance?" It is 144 Arkansas Razorbacks in one room.

University of Texas Medical School After years of research and millions of dollars, the UT Med School has finally announced the perfection of the artificial appendix.

Southern Methodist How many SMU coeds does it take to change a flat? Two, one to hold the drinks and one to call daddy.

Arkansas Did you hear about the Arkansas Razorback who signed up for the organ donor program? When he had to have a tooth pulled, he sent it to the Baylor school of dentistry.

Oklahoma What do you say to an Oklahoma Sooner in a three-piece suit? "How do you plead?"

Arkansas The University of Arkansas has announced a major new research project. They will be trying to mate an octopus with a cow to produce the world's first self-milker.

Houston Do you know what copulate is at the University of Houston? That's what they say when the police don't arrive on time.

Southern Methodist Do you know why SMU coeds are called Appendix? Because it costs so much to take them out.

Oklahoma Did you hear that Oklahoma has a lot of honor students? They go around practicing "Yes, Your Honor, No your Honor."

University of Texas Four graduates of the University of Texas had not seen each other for twenty years until they attended their class reunion. After a few too many drinks, they began telling some deep dark secrets on themselves.

The first one, who was a famous lawyer, admitted that for the previous ten years he had had a serious drinking problem but was able to keep it a secret from the world. The second, a world-famous heart surgeon, admitted that he had once been arrested for child molesting. The third, a former officer in a Texas Savings and Loan, admitted he had gambled away a lot of his depositors' money in Las Vegas.

When it came time for the fourth one to speak up he refused, saying he had no secrets. "Oh come on now," urged the other three, "everyone has some secret. We shared ours so now it's your turn."

After a moment's thought, the fourth one shook his head. "The only thing I can think of," he said, "is that I'm a compulsive gossip."

Oklahoma Did you hear about the Oklahoma Sooner who had to be cut from the football team? The only thing he couldn't do with a football was autograph it.

University of Texas The Aggie was out on a date with a coed from the University of Texas. When he took her to the door at the end of the evening, he naturally asked for a kiss.

"I don't kiss on the fist date," replied the lady Longhorn.

The Aggie thought for a moment then said, "Well, how about on the last date?"

Texas Tech The Red Raider freshman was anxious to have a car for his first year but his dad refused. "Son, I got along fine without a car and so can you."

"But Dad, all the kids have one." the Red Raider pleaded.

"I don't care about the other kids. Cars are too dangerous."

"But I'm a good driver," the son assured his obstinate father.

"That's not the kind of trouble I'm talking about."

"What then?" asked the student.

"How old are you?" the dad countered.

"I'm nineteen, why?" the son answered somewhat confused.

"If I'd had a car when I was in college, you'd be twenty-three right now."

Arkansas Razorback The Aggie and his Arkansas Razorback friend were on a hunting trip out in the Big Bend area when they got separated. After searching for hours, the Aggie was about to give up when he heard several shots. He ran in the direction of the gunfire and found his friend calmly reloading his rifle.

"Did you get a deer?" asked the Aggie. The Razorback shook his head.

"Oh, was it a sheep?" continued the Aggie. Again the Arkansas student shook his head.

After running through the list of every known game animal in the Lone Star State, the Aggie gave up. "Well what did you shoot?"

"A moose," the Razorback sharpshooter replied proudly.

"A moose?" the Aggie replied. "We don't have any moose in Texas."

"Well, you had at least one," the Razorback replied, "'cause I heard him moo just before I fired."

13

Texas Sports

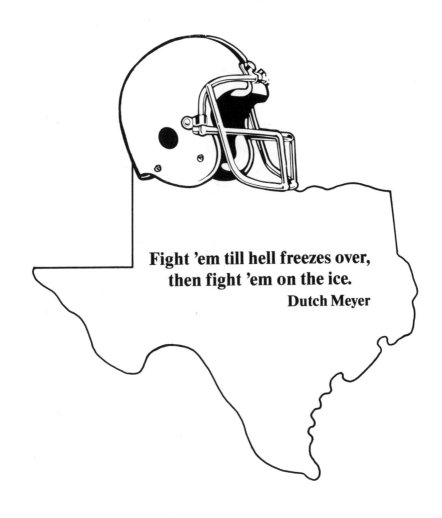

**Fight 'em till hell freezes over,
then fight 'em on the ice.**
Dutch Meyer

Whether you enjoy football, baseball, basketball, soccer, golf, tennis, boxing, auto racing, volley ball, hand ball, horseshoes, or even horse racing, you can find it in Texas (in the case of horse racing, you will be able to find it soon). And to be sure, Texans take their sports about as serious as they take money and pretty girls. But, as with any other aspect of Lone Star life, there is always some room for laughter with a little wisdom thrown in for good measure.

Say it Ain't So, Coach Pete Gent, the one-time Dallas Cowboy receiver, gave the world the infamous book *North Dallas Forty*. He also gave us one of the best Cowboys stories.

It seems Dallas had gone up to New York and gotten beat. On the plane ride home Coach Landry was going over strategy for the following week and he decided to switch Gent from the left side of the line to the right. Once the decision was made, Coach Landry went to the back of the plane, found Gent, and informed him, "Next week you're going to play on the other side of the line."

Without missing a beat, the quick-witted Gent replied, "You mean, coach, that I'm going to play for Philadelphia?"

Oldest of All Texas Boxing Jokes A young boxer was in his first fight at the arena in Fort Worth. It was soon apparent that the boy was no match for the other more experienced fighter. When the battered boxer reeled into his corner at the end of the first round, his trainer tried to keep up the fighter's confidence. "You're doing great; he ain't laid a hand on you," he said. The next round was even worse than the first, but the boy was game and lasted it out. As he returned to his corner, his trainer assured him, "You're beating him bad; he still ain't laid a glove on you."

The process continued through several rounds, each time the trainer assuring the boxer he was doing well. Finally, after the seventh round the bruised and bleeding young man barely managed to stagger back to his corner. When the trainer assured him the other guy still hadn't laid a hand on him, the young man looked up through his only eye that was still open and pleaded, "Then you better keep your eye on the referee this next round cause somebody is beatin' the hell out a me!"

The Rest of the Story: When the referee finally stopped the fight in the eighth round, the young man collapsed in the center of the ring. His trainer rushed to his side and, while treating his wounds, assured the young man, "If it's the last thing I do, I'm gonna get you a rematch with that guy."

Astrodomania When Houston's Astrodome first opened in 1965, it was quite an event. A local sports writer claimed it was what God would have built if he had the money. Evangelist Billy Graham, present for the opening, claimed the structure was the eighth wonder of the world. Years later Bud Adams, owner of the Oilers, would comment that if the Astrodome was the eighth wonder of the world, the *rent* on the Astrodome was the ninth.

Some people don't know that when the Dome first opened it had windows in the roof and a real grass playing field. The theory was the window would let in enough light to keep the grass alive. It didn't work. But the windows did open new possibilities for coaches. Al Spangler, a former Astro player, observed, "Don't get into a slump here because they don't force you to take extra batting practice — they make you wash the widows."

When the real grass refused to live, it was replaced with the now famous, or infamous, synthetic grass called Astroturf. That may have solved the problem of the playing field surface but not everyone was happy. Richie Allen, a noted baseballer, observed, "I don't want to play on grass a horse won't eat."

Another "first" for the Dome occurred when torrential rains fell during a game, flooding all the streets outside and preventing fans from going home. Tony Kubeck, who was announcing the game, commented, "I've heard of rain outs but this is the first time I've ever heard of a rain in."

Speaking of rain, the lack of moisture inside the Astrodome caused some problems for former Oiler coach Bum Phillips. Bum, who was a pretty fair country coach and a good ol' boy to boot, was known for wearing his cowboy hat during games. However, he refused to wear a Stetson on the sidelines of the Astrodome because he said he didn't wear his hat indoors. When some asked why he considered the inside of the Dome to be indoors, Bum explained, "When it can't rain on you, you're indoors."

As long as the Dome stands, there will doubtless be more stories, but thanks to present coach Jerry Glanville, all Oiler fans now know the real advantage of playing home games in the Dome. On a 1988 edition of *Inside the NFL*, Glanville shared the secret. He said, "Our biggest advantage in playing in the dome is probably the size of our Texas cockroaches. Some of the players from up north have never seen anything like that. They're as big as alligators. We have cockroaches so big in the visitors' dressing room, I've heard players say they rode 'em out to the bus."

Good Questions Houston Astro pitcher Larry Anderson, somewhat of a clubhouse philosopher, has asked some questions on the mysteries of life that are difficult to answer:

How can you tell when you are running out of invisible ink?
What do they call coffee breaks at the Lipton Tea Company?
Why does sour cream have an expiration date?
How come slim chance and fat chance mean the same thing?

Somebody Get a Tape Measure Raymond Berry, the pass catching wizard out of Paris, Texas and SMU, was once a coach for the Dallas Cowboys. When the team went to Thousand Oaks, California for training camp, Berry, who Tom Landry claimed invented the art of running precise pass patterns, was having trouble demonstrating his routes. "Something's wrong," he said, "I think the field is too narrow."

When they measured, it was found that the field used for years by Cal Lutheran and the Cowboys was, indeed, almost a foot too narrow.

Space-Age Recruiting When Tommy Nobis, the great linebacker out of the University of Texas, was trying to decide on whether to sign with Atlanta or Houston, he received some heavenly advice. Astronaut Frank Borman, who was orbiting the earth at the time, radioed back to earth, "Tell Nobis to sign with Houston." It didn't work, Nobis signed with Atlanta of the NFL. When told of Nobis' decision, Borman replied "There's no joy in Mudville."

One reason Nobis was so highly recruited was his outlook on how the game should be played. He said, "If you hustle, you don't have time to get tired. When you start thinking of yourself is when you start to hurt the team. You've got to get it out of your head you can't make it. You've got to get it in your head that you can."

Best Answer to a Stupid Sports Question After the Chicago Bears had thrashed the Washington Redskins 73 to 0, a sports writer asked Sammy Baugh, the Washington quarterback, what he thought would have happened if a Redskin receiver had not dropped a pass in the end zone. Baugh, now a Texas rancher, replied, "It would have been 73 to 7."

No Way to Talk About a President's Son When Eddie Childs was having difficulty selling his beloved Texas Rangers, he said, "I'll try to sell, but sooner or later there aren't going to be any suckers left out there." Some time later he did sell, to a group that included George W. Bush, son of the President.

Wanna Bet? Horse racing has only recently been legalized in Texas. But betting on horse racing has been a popular sport in Texas from the beginning of time. And the betting hasn't always been on the up and up.

Not long ago there was going to be a special race between four top Texas horses. Billy Fred and Bubba were in a bar having a drink and talking about the upcoming race. "I'll bet you $50 that Steeldust wins that race," Bubba said.

"I'll take that bet," Billy Fred replied. "Let's drink to it."

The men had a drink and then another and then another. Bubba got to feeling his oats and offered to up the bet to $500 and Billy Fred accepted. After a few more drinks, Bubba wanted to raise the bet to $5,000.

"I'll take that bet but I guarantee you're gonna loose," Billy Fred said.

"And how do you know?" asked Bubba.

"Because, I own Steeldust."

Bubba thought for a moment then said, "Well, it looks like we're in for the slowest race in history."

"How ya' figure it?" asked Billy Fred.

"Because," answered Bubba, "me and my brother, we own the other three horses."

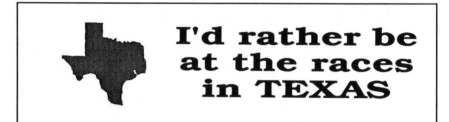

I'd rather be at the races in TEXAS

Until recently, pari-mutual betting on horse racing was against the law in Texas. As a result, Texans who enjoyed putting down a few shekels on the nose of some horse had to venture outside the state, and many of them drove cars with this bumper sticker in plain sight.

Speaking of horse racing, surely you've heard about the Texan who showed up at Louisiana Downs one day and entered his horse in a race. When he filled out the entry form, he listed the horses age as "at least" 7 years. "That's mighty old for a horse to be racing isn't it?," asked one of the judges.

"Naw, that old Texas horse will do ok," replied the Texan as he left to bet everything he had on his horse to win.

Naturally everyone thought the Texan had lost his mind and they bet heavily against the seven year old. But to everyone's surprise but the Texan, the seven year old came out of the gate first, led all the way, and finished ten lengths ahead of the field.

After the race, track officials suspected foul play and challenged the Texan. "That horse ran mighty fast for being seven years old. Why haven't you ever raced him before?"

"Because," replied the Texan, "It took me and all my hands more than four years to catch him and then it took us almost three years more to break him for riding."

Thanks Tex Pom Poms were once the things to shake at football games. But the Dallas Cowboy Cheerleaders have come up with something better. Thanks to Tex Schramm for inventing them (the cheerleaders, that is).

The Right Attitude Jerry Glanville explained his Oiler's attitude toward playing: "We don't care if we're 50 points ahead or 50 points behind. We're going to play a hundred miles an hour, try to get in on every play, with every single player. That kind of football no man should apologize for."

What Happened to Lethal Injections? On September 18, 1988, the New York Jets whipped the Houston Oilers 45 to 3. Following the game, a dejected and upset Jerry Glanville said, "Somebody is going to pay for this hanging."

Famous Cowboy Quote Walt Garrison, a real cowboy who played football for the Dallas Cowboys, was responsible for one of the most often repeated quotes about Tom Landry. When asked if he ever saw the coach smile, Garrison replied, "I don't know. I only played there nine years."

Rest of the Story: While the above quote has often been repeated, it is not complete. In his book *Once a Cowboy,* Garrison said the last line of the quote should be, "But I know he smiled a least three times cause he has three kids."

The Versatile Back Walt Garrison, whom the *Dallas Morning News* referred to as "the Will Rogers of professional football," was the subject of one of the most famous Dallas Cowboy quotes. When asked about the versatility of Garrison, Don Meredith replied, "If you needed four yards, you'd give the ball to Garrison and he'd get four yards. If you needed twenty yards, you'd give the ball to Garrison and he'd get four yards."

Marriage Made in Heaven Don Meredith is also responsible for perhaps the most famous quote, by a player, about coach Landry. "Tom Landry is a perfectionist," Dandy Don said. "If he was married to Racquel Welch, he'd expect her to cook."

Image Breaker Another Meredith classic quote concerned legendary quarterback Roger Stauback, who was known for being a fine upstanding citizen as well as outstanding quarterback. "We're going to have to do something about this guy. He's going to ruin the image of an NFL quarterback if he doesn't start smoking, drinking, cussing, or something."

Number 1 in Your Heart Meredith, who always said he was number 17 in your program and number 1 in your heart, offered his most famous quote during a nationally televised game, and it didn't concern either a coach or a player. As a TV camera scanned the crowd, the cameraman settled on a solitary fan sitting near the top of the stands. Apparently the man wasn't impressed with being on television because he just looked up at the camera and nonchalantly "shot the finger" to America. After a moment's hesitation, Meredith quipped, "Well, I guess he's saying we're still number one."

Hall of Fame Philosophy Mean Joe Green out of Temple, Texas and North Texas State University (and the Pittsburgh Steelers) once said: "There is no such thing as hitting too hard."

Ruined Ending Pete Gent, the former Dallas Cowboy who wrote *North Dallas Forty,* once happened on a rookie reading the Cowboy playbook. "Don't bother reading it kid," Gent advised, "Everybody gets killed in the end."

Wrong Places, Right Times Chuck Howley, one of the most popular and proficient linebackers ever to play for the Dallas Cowboys, once said, "There's a real irony in my life. When I look back on all the really big plays I've made in my career, I realize I've always been out of position when I made them."

Best Excuse for Losing a Football Game According to Bob Hayes, the reason Dallas lost a 1969 play-off game to Cleveland was, "We were playing on a wet field and they were playing on a dry field."

Gone But Not Forgotten Joe Don Looney, who was killed in a 1988 motorcycle accident, was one of the wildest football players ever to come out of Texas. After playing for several college teams, Joe Don ended up with Oklahoma. Following college he played pro ball for a short time, and some of his antics are almost legendary:

On how to run with the ball, he said, "Anybody can run where the hole is. A good football player makes his own holes."

After practice, Joe Don refused to put his socks in the bin labeled socks, his athletic supporter in the bin labeled jocks, and so on because, as he explained, "I don't believe in signs."

On relationships, he observed, "I never met a man I didn't like except Will Rogers."

When the coach asked him to take a message in to the quarterback, Joe Don replied, "If you want a messenger, call Western Union."

After a good punt, Joe Don remarked, "How'd you like that one, God?"

Fellow Texan George Sauer may have put Joe Don Looney into perspective when he said, "Never was a man more aptly named."

Lemonade Abe Lemons, onetime colorful basketball coach at the University of Texas, has moved on to other opportunities. Before departing, Abe gave us some pearls of sports wisdom:

"Just once I'd like to see the win-loss records of doctors right out in front where people could see them — won ten, lost three, tied two."

"I'd rather be a football coach. That way you only lose eleven games a year."

When asked if he jogs, Lemons replied, "Hell no. When I die I want to be sick."

Landry Tom Landry, the only head coach the Dallas Cowboys have ever fired (so far) is now retired to the good life. He left behind wonderful memories and some words of wisdom, of which the following is a small sample:

"I try not to get frustrated over things I don't have much to do with."

"A team that has character doesn't need stimulation."

"You must first know offense before you can coach defense."

"You never know when you'll be surrounded by Redskins."

"Nothing funny ever happens on a football field."

Landry Levity Although generally known as all business, those who know him best swear Tom Landry has a humorous if not downright funny side. Among the many stories of his humor, the best may have occurred in 1973. The Cowboys were playing in New York. Some prankster phoned in to say there was a bomb in the press box. It never materialized and after the game, one of the writers asked Landry what would have happened if the press box had blown up. He replied, "We would have observed thirty seconds of silence and then continued the game with great enthusiasm."

Putting it in Perspective In 1981, Houston Oiler quarterback Kenny Stabler had a great game against the dreaded Pittsburgh Steelers but the team still lost. After the game, Stabler put his performance into perspective: "It doesn't matter when you lose. It's like earrings on a pig. It doesn't make a whole lot of difference."

Somebody Get a Rope The most famous play in Cotton Bowl history occurred in the 1950 game between Rice and Alabama. As Rice's Dickie Maegle streaked toward a touchdown, Alabama's Tommy Lewis came off the bench and tackled him. The referee managed to prevent a riot by awarding a touchdown to Rice. At halftime, Maegle commented, "I've read books about Texas and I guess they'll hang me from the goal posts in the second half." Fortunately, clear heads prevailed and there was no hanging.

Bobby Layne, shown here as a young Texas Longhorn, was perhaps the best quarterback Texas has ever produced. He was known far and wide for his escapades on and off the field. He was also known for a quick wit. Some examples include:

"I want to run out of money and breath at the same time."
"If a man works after noon, the job is too big for him in the first place."
"You don't need much sleep if you sleep fast."

Scholar Athlete When one of his players received four F's and one D, Texas A&M coach Shelby Metcalf commented, "Son, looks to me like you're spending too much time on one subject."

The Mad Bomber In a 1974 game between the Dallas Cowboys and the Washington "Dreadskins," Roger Staubach went down with an injury and most fans thought the hopes of the 'Pokes went with him. Then off the bench came a former rattlesnake hunter out of Abilene Christian College named Clint Longley. Incredibly, the unheralded rookie lead the Cowboys to one of their greatest comeback victories in history. Following the game, Blaine Nye had a perfect explanation for the near miracle: "It was a triumph of the uncluttered mind."

Apparently, Longley's mind soon became cluttered. He ultimately got into a fight with Roger "the Dodger" and soon found himself out of the Cowboy organization. He was hardly ever heard of again.

Sure Shots Texas golf legend Byron Nelson said, "The only shots you can be dead sure of are those you've already had."

How's That Again? When the Houston Oilers were preparing for the 1972 season, then coach Bill Petersen encouraged the team, "Men I want you to remember one word and only one word this year. Super Bowl."

Bumisms Oail "Bum" Phillips was one of the most popular coaches in Texas history. Not only could he coach, he could think and talk. A lot of what came out of his mouth is priceless:

"The thing that decides the size of your funeral is the weather."

"They say familiarity breeds contempt. I don't believe that. I know my mother better than anyone and I don't have contempt for her."

"I'd hate to have a guy who had to have a pep talk to get him to play."

"Do all you can, then do a little more. That's all there is to it."

"Pari-mutual wagering means lots of jobs. Texas needs pari-mutual betting. Besides, that way we don't have so far to drive.

"When I was a kid, our land was so poor we had to fertilize the house to raise the windows."

On why he doesn't use stop watches: "What do you have to time Billy "Whiteshoes" Johnson or Kenny Burrough for? They're fast enough."

"Two kinds of football players ain't worth a damn. One that never does what he's told and the other that never does anything except what he's told."

"Friendship is nothing you can take from a guy. He's got to give it."

On why he didn't scrimmage his players against each other: "Houston's not on our schedule."

"There are two types of coaches. Them that have just been fired and them that are going to be fired."

"The film looks suspiciously like the game itself."

"The behinder we got, the worse it got."

"Pickup trucks is one of the five things I know something about. That and cold beer, BBQ'd ribs, gumbo, and chewin' tobacco."

Roasted Bum At a recent roast for Bum Phillips, one of the featured speakers was Ann Richards, the Texas state treasurer. She sort of put things into perspective when she closed her speech. "Now, all I can say, Bum, is that football is a helluva way to make a living. And I know you're glad to be out of it and into something real simple like ranching, where you can deal with the front end of horses. But I understand why you love it. After all, you know what they say. Politics is a lot like football. You have to be smart enough to play the game and dumb enough to think it's important.

How's That Again? Mickey Rivers, former player for the Rangers, once explained his goals for the upcoming season: "My goal this season is to hit .300, score 100 runs, and stay injury prone."

It was also Rivers who once started a trivia contest with the following question: "What is the name of that dog in Rin Tin Tin?"

The Greatest Cowboy Story Ever Told In the late 1950s, Clint Murchison realized that the NFL was about to blossom into something big and he wanted an expansion team for Dallas. There was only one problem. George Preston Marshall, owner of the Washington Redskins disliked Murchison and opposed a franchise for Dallas. But Clint was not to be denied.

Although the details of the story vary, Murchison learned that the rights to the song "Hail to the Redskins" were for sale by the composer. Murchison, in a move that would warm the heart of J. R. Ewing, purchased the song and then informed Marshall that he couldn't play the beloved song at Redskin games — couldn't, that is, unless Marshall was willing to vote yes when the subject of a Dallas franchise came up for a vote at the league meeting. The ploy worked; Murchison was awarded the franchise and the Redskins got their song back.

How's That Again? In 1980, members of the Dallas Cowboys squared off against the cheerleaders on the television game show Family Feud. Harvey Martin was asked: What invention of the 20th century are you most thankful for? He replied, "Since this is women, the 20th century, I'll say bra."

Larry Cole was asked: Name a vegetable people stuff? He replied, "Watermelon."

Seeing Red, the Hard Way Louise Ritter, the high jumping Dallas lady, made it to the finals at the Seoul Olympics. When she noticed the other finalists were 2 Bulgarians, 2 Soviets, and a Romanian, she said, "Gosh, it's just me and the communists." But Louise held fast and struck a blow for democracy by winning. Afterwards, when asked if she was disappointed about not setting a world record in the process of winning, she replied, "I'd like to get a world record, but you can always be a former world record holder. You can never be a former Olympic gold medalist."

Royalty Speaks Darrell Royal gave us many pearls of wisdom during his years at Texas. Here's a sampling:
"There is no laughter in losing."
"If a player is the least bit confused, he can't be aggressive. Tattoo that on your wall. Or better still, on your wallet. You must play aggressive football to win, and you cannot be aggressive and confused at the same time."
"You never lose a game if your opponent doesn't score."
"Punt returns will kill you before a minnow can swim a dipper."
"It's no disgrace to get knocked down as long as you get back up."
"Ya' gotta dance with who brung ya."

How's That Again? Darrell Royal, former head coach of the Texas Longhorns, was once asked about the lack of speed of one of his players. Coach Royal replied "He doesn't have a whole lot of speed but maybe Elizabeth Taylor can't sing."

He Certainly Should! When the No. 1 Texas Longhorns were preparing to play the No. 2 Arkansas Razorbacks for the 1969 national championship, the churches in Little Rock, where the game was to be played, displayed signs encouraging the Hogs on to victory. When asked his opinion, Texas coach Royal replied, "God should be neutral." As the game turned out, God may not have been neutral. Some claim the Horns had heavenly help in coming from behind to win 15 to 14 in one of the most exciting college games ever played.

Another Neutrality Question When Grant Teaff was named coach of the Baylor Bears he was given a plaque with the following inscription: God grant Teaff the serenity to accept the things he cannot change, the courage to change the things he can and the wisdom to have us in the Cotton Bowl in a couple of years."

His isn't Always Neutral In 1956, the Texas Aggies upset the heavily favored Texas Longhorns. The Aggie coach at the time, Paul "Bear" Bryant explained the game, "It went according to prayer."

What About a Sack? One of Darrell Royal's most famous quotes: "I've always felt that three things can happen to you whenever you throw the football, and two of them are bad. You can throw it incomplete or have it intercepted." Apparently he never considered the possibility of his quarterback being sacked.

But Can She Cook? The Texas Longhorns once won a game despite some sloppy play. After the game, Coach Royal summed up his feelings, "Ol' ugly is better than ol' nothing."

Best Excuse for Missing a Field Goal After former Dallas Cowboy Rafeal Septian's missed field goal, he explained, "The ball was upside down."

Second Best Excuse for Missing a Field Goal On another occasion, Rafeal Septian explained a miss at Texas Stadium with, "The grass was too tall." Texas Stadium has artificial turf.

Still Fastest After All These Years "Bullet" Bob Hayes was billed as the "World's Fastest Human" when drafted by the Dallas Cowboys. After his football career ended, Hayes ran afoul of the law and was sentenced to jail. With a little good behavior, he was released after a few months, prompting *Dallas Morning News* sports columnist Blackie Sherrod to report, "Bob Hayes has proven he's still the worlds fastest human by doing a five-year prison sentence in nine months."

How's That Again? Tex Schramm, longtime general manager of the Dallas Cowboys, is now head of World Wide American Football League (already being called Waffle). One of his most famous quotes is, "Sometimes you win in the first year under a new coach on enthusiasm and vitality and newness alone. It's kind of high unto itself. But, then, you have to find a way to keep it up when the romance is trailing off. That's the hard part. In football or any other marriage."

Lee Trevino, the happy-go-lucky former Texas golf hustler who turned golf millionaire, once said, "We all leak a little oil but the good ones control the flow."

Fightin' Words Lee Trevino started out as a caddy and worked his way up to golf hustler, often challenging opponents with a Dr Pepper bottle. He worked and played hard and eventually became one of the state's most loved players. However, he could have gotten into some serious trouble after winning his first major tournament. He said, "I'm so happy, I'm gonna buy the Alamo and give it back to Mexico."

His Turn Lee Trevino was once struck by lightning while out on the golf course. Although he wasn't hurt too severely, his perspective changed. "When God wants to play through," he said, "you let him play through."

Trevino's method of playing also changed. "When I'm on a course and it starts to rain and lightning, I hold up my one iron cause I know even God can't hit a one iron."

How's That Again? More famous quotes from Lee Trevino:
"The older I get, the better I used to be."
"I was already nine years old when I was born."
"You can talk to a fade, but a hook won't listen."

Makes Sense Duane Thomas, who didn't talk much while with the Dallas Cowboys, did come up with one very interesting question concerning the Super Bowl. He said, "It isn't the ultimate game. If it was they wouldn't be playing it next year."

Lingering Questions Duane Thomas was responsible for the famous description of Texas E. Schramm. "Schramm is a liar, thief, and crook," said Duane. When told of the quote, Schramm replied, "Two out of three ain't bad." Unfortunately, Tex never explained which two Duane got right.

Tell Me Too The Dallas Cowboy Cheerleaders have achieved much fame, and unless the Jay Birds cut them, they will continue to be an integral part of the Dallas home games. When Viktor Tikhonov, coach of the Russian national hockey team, saw the cheerleaders during an exhibition tour in the United States, he asked, "Tell me, these women, are they wayward?"

Perfect Pitching Staff When knuckleballer Charlie Hough was the recognized ace of the staff, Texas Ranger manager Bobby Valentine once described his perfect pitching staff. "I always have preferred two lefties and two righties with Charlie; two lefties, two righties and a neuter."

Call the Cops Too For most of his career, Randy White was known as the football player's football player. He enjoyed a magnificent career with the Cowboys and was known for being able to play despite the pain of small injuries. Once, when the 'Pokes were playing the Washington "Dreadskins," Randy didn't get up after a play. Teammate Charlie Waters, instantly concerned, ran up to the referee and demanded, "You better check these guys for knives."

How's That Again? In 1988, then Texas Ranger Mitch Williams had some trouble with the Boston Red Socks. It seems the Socks thought

Mitch had thrown a little close to Wade Boggs. To show their displeasure and to try and intimidate Williams, the Boston players all stood up on the steps of the dugout. After the game, Williams was asked if he was worried. He replied, "I've been in fights before and I've been beaten up by littler guys than they have."

Lights, Camera, Action The 1962 AFL Championship game between the Dallas Texans and the Houston Oilers was one of the longest games in football history. When regulation play ended with the teams tied, the coaches prepared for overtime. Since a coin flip would decide who got the ball first, Hank Stramm, the Texans coach, took Abner Haynes aside and explained, "If they win the toss and elect to receive, we'll kick to the clock."

Abner nodded and trotted out on the field for the toss. As a national television audience watched and listened, the referee pitched the coin into the air. Dallas won the toss and the ref asked Haynes for his choice.

"We'll kick to the clock." Abner said, apparently excited.

"Come again?" asked Referee Harold "Red" Bourne.

"We'll kick to the clock." Abner Haynes repeated his choice.

"You can either call the kickoff or which goal to defend, but not both." Referee Bourne said, explaining the options to Abner Haynes.

"We'll kick." Abner Haynes, frustrated and excited, had won the toss and still elected to kick.

Al Jamieson, the stunned Houston Captain, quickly said, "We'll take the wind." Incredibly, Haynes had given the Oilers both the ball and the wind in the Championship game. Fortunately for the health and well being of Abner Haynes, Dallas still won the game.

Going Out in Style Doak Walker, the Heisman Trophy winner from SMU, abruptly retired from professional football when only twenty-eight years old. He explained, "I want to get out while I still have all my teeth and both my knees."

Football is a Business Back when the World Football League was still in existence, then Cowboy owner Clint Murchison, Jr., commented, "If the World Football League succeeds, I'm not going after their players; I'm going after their accountants."

Note to Jerry Jones: It was also Murchison who said of football ownership, "You could make more money investing in government bonds, but football is more fun."

Always Remember Bones Irvin, an assistant to "Bear" Bryant at Texas A&M, said "Some days you can't block 'em, some days you can't tackle 'em, but there is never a day you can't fight 'em."

Best Advice Texan Babe Didrickson Zaharris, probably the greatest woman athlete ever born, offered two pieces of advice which hold true today. For lady golfers, Babe said, "You've got to loosen your girdle and really let the ball have it." For anyone playing any game, she said, "If a game is worth playing, it's worth playing to win."

Original Oil Spill Early Dallas Cowboy Tom Franckhauser, commenting on the team's depth, said: "We had some talented players, but just not enough of them. We were a lot like an oil slick; we came from everywhere but we weren't very deep."

Contributor Dave Brownfield swears this is a true story. As he tells it, Bo Rollins, a longtime Texas coach who doubled as a teacher, once suspected two of his students were cheating. He got his proof after giving a test when one of the boys answered a difficult question with "I don't know." The other boy answered the same question with "me either."

Best Sports Question Ever Asked The year after the Texas Rangers traded Len Barker to the Cleveland Indians, Barker surprised the baseball world by pitching what was thought to be a perfect game. However, *Dallas Morning News* sports columnist Randy Galloway challenged the result with a question that has yet to be answered: "How could it have been a perfect game? It was in Cleveland."

This is Not an Aggie Joke! It happened during the Texas A&M - Houston basketball game in the 1993 SWC tournament. Midway through the second half the Aggies received their third technical foul of the game. Texas A&M radio announcer Dave South had seen enough of what he thought was poor officiating. He grabbed his neck in a mock "choking" sign directed toward Bryan Stout, a Southwest Conference official working the game. Stout apparently had also seen enough. Acting fully within his rights as an official, Stout ejected South from the game, marking the first time in SWC history that a radio announcer was thrown out of a game.

From Death Valley Days to Happy Days Again

When Arkansas millionaire Jerry Jones anted up 140 million dollars to buy the Dallas Cowboys from Bum Bright, the sports life of Dallas, Texas was forever changed. First of course, there was the poorly handled dismissal of Tom Landry, the only coach the Cowboys had ever had before Jones. Then there was a general house cleaning at Valley Ranch and many familiar faces were gone. And then there was the less-than-spectacular 1-15 inaugural season. The folks around Dallas began to refer to Valley Ranch as "Death Valley" Ranch and Texas

began to refer to Valley Ranch as "Death Valley" Ranch and Texas Stadium looked a lot like the Temple of Doom. Bashing Jones, the apparent country bumpkin, and Jimmy Johnson, the upstart college coach, became the real sport in Dallas. Funny how much things can change in four short years. Now, Jerry Jones is widely thought to be able to walk on water.

Tarnish on Jerry Jones' Silver Tongue   In the beginning, Jerry Jones was somewhat less than polished. He apparently didn't have a clue about dealing with the media. Here's some of the more classic foot-in-mouth Jerry Jones comments. *I'll be in charge of everything from socks to jocks* — Jones later said he just meant that he would be a full time owner involved in the day-to-day operations. *Troy looks good in the showers* — Jones was actually reverting to his earlier playing days when coaches would say this or that player might look good in the shower but that doesn't mean he can play. *They're the pick of the litter* — What there is of the Texas stadium roof almost caved in on Jones for this comment about the Cowboy's cheerleaders.

Jerry Jones the Prognosticator   Some things that Jones said which were thought to be humorous at the time turned out not to be. In his first news conference, he announced to the world, "We must win. We will win." There were plenty of skeptics at the time but they are mighty hard to find these days.

Jimmy Johnson the Prognosticator   The losses were mounting every week in 1989 and the future looked dismal. Then suddenly, without warning, the Cowboys beat the Washington Redskins for their only victory of the season. Following the game, Johnson was asked for the significance of the victory. Although pleased, the coach offered a bit of prophecy when he said, "We are going to have bigger wins." He was right, just ask Buffalo.

That's a Dumb Rule   Elizabeth Taylor came to Dallas and Jerry Jones invited her to participate in the coin toss to begin a Cowboy game. Liz said sure, why not. At game time, the officials, the captains of both teams, Mr. Jones and Ms. Taylor, and several photographers gathered at midfield. The referee tossed the coin and Liz made the call as planned. But there was a problem. When the result of the call gave Dallas the ball, the captain of the other team protested, loudly. Seems everyone, the referee included, was so dazzled by the presence of Ms. Taylor that they forgot the captain of the visiting team is the one who calls the coin toss. When the oversight was angrily pointed out to the ref, the toss was redone.

Are the Cowboys Really God's Team? There is an old story which claims the famous hole in the roof of Texas Stadium was left there so God could look down on Sundays and watch his team play. That may or may not be true but it is a fact that on the Friday before the Cowboys played the San Francisco 49ers in the NFC championship game, the bay area was rocked by an earthquake measuring 5.7 on the Richter scale. When asked to comment, Jimmy Johnson replied, "I felt it but I thought it was just because the Cowboys had come to town."

No All-Texas Super Bowl When both the Dallas Cowboys and Houston Oilers made the playoffs in 1992, some people, admittedly most of them were Texans, began to dream of a possible Super Bowl involving both professional football teams from the Lone Star state. Alas, it was not to be, thanks to the Oilers caving in like a soap bubble under a brick. The Oilers blew a 32 point lead in the second half of their game against Buffalo, the team that ultimately lost to Dallas in the Super Bowl by 35 points. Following the season the Oilers promptly fired two coaches but kept Jack Pardee as head coach. One Houston sports writer commented that firing the two coaches in an effort to solve the Oiler's problems was much like using a band-aid to cure a decapitation.

Lett's Legacy It was late in the fourth quarter of Super Bowl XXVII. The outcome was no longer in question. Jim Jeffcoat burst through the Buffalo line and sacked Frank Reich causing a fumble. Leon Lett scooped up the ball and set sail for the Buffalo goal line 65 yards away. After 64 yards he started celebrating. Unfortunately, Don Beebe of the Bills ran down Lett at the one yard line and knocked the ball free. The ball bounced into and out of the end zone for a touchback. So, instead of a touchdown for the Cowboys, the Bills got the ball back at their own 20 yard line. Of course, one more touchdown wouldn't have changed the outcome, but it did make one difference. Had Lett scored, the Cowboys would have had 59 points, which would have been a Super Bowl record. Oh well, there's always next year, right Leon?

What About Tail Lights? Following the victory in Super Bowl XXVII, Cowboy wide receiver Michael Irvin was asked about the ring each member of the winning team would receive. "I've already told them I want diamonds in my ring bigger than headlights," Irvin replied. "I want diamonds so big I can turn off the headlights when I'm driving down the road, stick my hand out the window and still be able to see."

This Guy Must Be From New York When Dallas squared off against Buffalo in Super Bowl XXVII, Texas Governor Ann Richards placed a friendly wager with Mario Cuomo, the governor of New York. Miss Richards put up a year's supply of Texas jalepeno peppers against 1,000

Buffalo wings. Simple enough, right? Unfortunately there was some confusion and apparently some anxious moments for Mr. Cuomo. He thought the bet was that if Dallas won the game then he had to *personally* eat all the peppers, a thought that surely would bring tears to the eyes of the strongest Texan. Fortunately for the New York governor, all he had to do was provide the wings and his sigh of relief could be heard all the way to Austin.

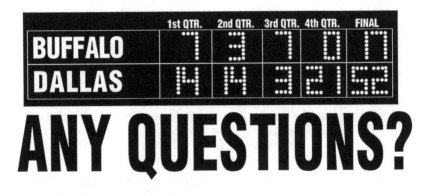

ANY QUESTIONS?

Maybe There are Some Questions   Following the Cowboy victory, the above headline and graphic appeared in the *Dallas Morning News*. While the headline seems to say it all, a lot of people around Texas, especially in Dallas, do have a couple of questions. The first is, does the "D" in Big D stand for Dallas or Dynasty? The second question perhaps says a lot about Texans being fickle fans and loving a winner. Not long after the victory in Super Bowl XXVII, two sports fans were overheard in a bar discussing the relative merits of the Cowboy organization. At one point the conversation stopped for a few moments when neither could think of the answer to the question, "What was the name of that guy who used to coach the Cowboys?"

14

Worm Drowning

**Some of the biggest fish in
Texas are caught by the tale.**

A lot of people don't know it, but Texas has more lakes than Minnesota, which bills itself as the land of a thousand lakes. The truth is, of all the states, only that "A" state has more lakes than Texas. And you can bet, on most any weekend and a fair amount of week days, those lakes are crowded with fisherman because fishing has to be the greatest participant sport in Texas. There can be no greater target for levity than the poor ol' fisherman.

How Much? The old Texan was really laying it on to a small gathering of northerners at a convention. "Boys," the Texan said, "I'm tellin' you it was the biggest fish ever caught on earth with a rod and reel. And I caught it in a pond no bigger than this room. Why, when I landed that monster, the water level in the pond dropped ten feet. Beat all I ever saw."

"How much did he weigh?" asked one listener.

"Don't rightly know," the Texan explained, "we didn't have no scale that would hold that much. But I'll tell you this, while we were hooking that monster up to a crane so we could load him in an 18-wheel truck, the shadow of that fish fell across the scales. And boys, if I'm lyin' I'm dyin, the shadow of that fish weighed 12 pounds."

That old philosopher Az Tex observed: A fisherman ain't nuthin' but one jerk on the end of a line waitin' for a jerk on the other end.

It Didn't Pass A few years ago, a state senator who was an avid fisherman tried to get a bill passed requiring that fishing licenses and marriage licenses expire on the same date. When that failed, he tried to get a law passed requiring fisherman to marry their rods and get a yearly license to be married.

Kevin McCarthy, of KLIF radio in Dallas, has a favorite Stanley Marsh III story that is also somewhat of a fish tale. It seems Stanley was having trouble with poachers cleaning off his trot line. After several attempts to nab the perpetrators, Stanley turned loose his creative mind. And folks, no one in Texas has a more creative mind than Stanley Marsh III. He had a friend who worked in a research lab and Stanley managed to get several monkeys who had given their life for science. He outfitted each dead monkey in children-sized scuba gear and promptly hooked them on the trot line. Funny thing happened, Stanley never again had trouble with poachers.

Strange but True? Several camera companies have reported that 4 out of every 5 enlarging attachments they sell are shipped to Texas.

Sound Advice? Although many consider it an old wives' tale, some people swear the following is the best advice on judging when to go fishing:

If the wind is from the east, the fishing will be least
If the wind is from the west, the fishing will be best.

Sounds Reasonable The old fisherman was sitting on a bank next to a "No Fishing" sign doing his best to catch some fish. Unfortunately the game warden happened by. The fisherman immediately pulled up his line to expose a wiggling minnow on the hook and assured the warden, "Just teaching him to swim."

From the Texas Bumper Sticker Hall of Fame. Seen on a pickup near Lake Travis in Austin.

The highway patrolman pulled over an old fisherman. "You've got a broken tail light," the patrolman said. The fisherman immediately jumped out of his car and hurried to the back for a look. When he saw the broken light he fell to his knees and wept like a baby.

"Now hold on," exclaimed the trooper, "you shouldn't worry so about a broken tail light."

"I'm not," replied the fisherman. "I'm worried about what has become of the new bass boat I left home with."

Then there was the old fisherman who finally gave in and got married. About two weeks later, some bills arrived for purchases his new wife had made before they were married. "You don't mind, do you honey?" asked the bride.

"Hell yes, I mind," replied the fisherman. "That's like going fishing and asking the fish to buy the worms that caught him."

A sign that is perhaps the most ignored in Texas, other than speed limit signs is: No Fishing Allowed. One old farmer who didn't want anyone fishing on his private lake except family and friends finally got so disgusted with people ignoring his No Fishing sign that he went down to the printer and had a new one made up that ended all unauthorized fishing on his lake. It read:

Posted
Keep Out
Official State of Texas
Game and Fish Commission
Water Moccasin
Hatchery

Best Ever Texas Fishing Sign As you go toward Lake Lavon out of Wylie, Texas, a bait shop has a huge sign printed on a wall proclaiming: Our minnows are guaranteed to catch fish or die trying.

Is it Plagiarism? Michael Ray, a good friend from down in Houston, has the following sign hanging in his office:

If you wish to be happy for one day, get intoxicated.
If you wish to be happy for three days, get married.
If you wish to be happy for eight days, kill your pig and eat it.
If you wish to be happy forever, learn to fish.

Now the sign says it is an old Chinese proverb, but I'd bet the old Chinese prophet was really an East Texas bass fisherman.

F.A. Over in East Texas they've started an organization for men who just can't stop fishing. They call the organization Fishermen Anonymous. Whenever you feel the urge to fish, you call the support group and they send over several buddies to drink with you.

From the Texas Bumper Sticker Hall of Fame. Think about it, how many times have you said, "I wish I could go fishing?"

Did you hear about the South Texas rancher who had a twenty-five-acre private lake in his south pasture? He had the biggest basshole in Texas.

Surely you've heard about the Texas fisherman who went over to Russia to try his luck. When he returned, his friends naturally expected some fabulous tales but when asked how he did, the Texan simply replied, "Didn't catch a thing."
"How come?" asked the friends.
"You can't catch nuthin' in Russia," the Texan explained, "the fish are afraid to open their mouths."

Scientific Fact It is impossible to fish and worry at the same time.

Old fishermen never die, they just smell that way.

Growing Season In Texas, the fish seem to grow the most between the moment they strike a lure and the instant they spit it out.

And Justice for All The ol' Texas fisherman was having a wonderful time. He was catching more fish than the law would allow, literally. Sure enough, he got arrested by the game warden. When the fisherman was taken into court, the judge asked, "You are charged with catching 40 black bass over the limit. How do you plead?"
"Guilty your honor," replied the Texan.
"Very well, your fine is $150.00 and I hope that will be a lesson to you."
"Oh, it will your honor," replied the Texan. "But there is one other thing. Could I possibly get a dozen or so copies of the court records in this case?"

Ain't it the Truth The only thing that can make a man a bigger liar than fishing is the IRS.

A Good Lesson The youngster came running into Sunday school about fifteen minutes late. When asked to explain his tardiness, he replied, "I was gonna go fishing but Dad wouldn't let me."
"Well," the teacher said, "I congratulate your father. And I hope you learned something."
"I sure did, Ma'am," replied the little Texan. "Next time I'm gonna remind mother to buy plenty of bait so Dad'll take me along."

That old philosopher Az Tex once observed that the model wife is one who will save the worms when she digs in the garden. The perfect wife, on the other hand, is one that doesn't mind you digging in the garden for worms.

Sign in an East Texas bait house:

> Fishing is like sex.
> The next best thing to
> doing it is talking about it.

You Could Look it up in the Bible The farmer's wife was having a devil of a time. Her husband kept ignoring the fields in favor of going fishing. Finally, one day the husband came dragging in from a hard day on the lake and his wife sat him down at the kitchen table for a discussion.

"Can you tell me, dear," she asked, "why you always insist on going fishing?"

"Why, it's biblical, dear," he replied.

"Biblical? she asked, "How do you figure it?"

"Well, as you know, when the Lord created the earth he saw fit to cover three fourths of it with water and one fourth with land. Now, I don't know about you, but as far as I'm concerned, that was a clear signal that a man ought to spend at least three fourths of his time fishing and one fourth plowing. And I'm working hard to maintain my proper ratio."

Fisherman's Dilemma You are out on the lake and your wife, who can't swim, falls overboard at the moment a world record black bass strikes your lure.

You know a fisherman is getting old when minnow buckets hold more appeal than mini-skirts.

A Texas Classic Two old Texans were sitting around discussing their most unusual catches. "The most unusual thing I ever caught," said the first, "was a twenty-five pound pure white, albino black bass."

The other man thought for a moment, then replied, "The most unusual thing I ever caught was an old lantern."

"What's unusual about that?" asked the first.

"Well, after I got it in the boat and scrapped off the mud and silt, I found the lantern was still burning."

The first fisherman thought about that for a moment and offered a bargain. "Look," he said, "I'll take twenty pounds off my fish and add some color if you'll put out your light."

Another Texas Classic A group of men were sitting around swapping fish stories one day and everyone but the Texan had tried to outdo the others with a wild tale. But the Texan remained silent. Finally one of the others asked the Texan if he had fishing stories to relate. The Texan sort of hung his head as if ashamed. "I ain't got nuthin' to say," replied the Texan, "cause the last fish I caught was too small to keep."

"Oh, so you threw him back?" asked one of the others.

"Sure did," replied the Texan.

"Well how small was it?" asked another.

"That fish was so small," replied the Texan, "that it only took four of us to get it out of the boat and back into the water."

Sad but True Many a Texas fisherman has spent long hours on a lake and all he accomplished was the murder of a couple a dozen worms.

World's best excuse for being late getting home from a fishing trip: "Honey, I caught so many fish that the truck was overloaded and wouldn't go no more than five miles an hour. Now, I realized that would make me late so I started throwing out the fish one at a time. By the time I got up to full speed, all I had left was these three little fish."

A Safe Bet The old fisherman went down to the paper and asked to place an ad offering a reward of $1,000 for the return of his wife's cat. The man at the newspaper commented that $1,000 seemed a lot for one cat. "Not this one," replied the fisherman. "The last time I went out in my bass boat, I drowned the cat."

That old philosopher Az Tex once observed that it sure is strange how one little nibble can keep a man fishing for hours.

Just Like a Woman Did you hear about the Texas lady who can't make herself bait a hook, couldn't possibly take a fish off a hook if she caught one, flatly refuses to clean fish, and would rather go to the dentist than cook fish? Her favorite sport is fishing. Her name is Judy.

The fisherman and his wife were celebrating their golden wedding anniversary. One of the guests, noting that a fisherman is gone a lot, especially on weekends, asked the wife if she had ever considered divorce in their fifty years together. "Divorce?" answered the wife. "I never did consider divorce as I recall. But I do remember considering homicide on several occasions."

Something is Fishy A hospital over in East Texas had an emergency one day when their scale broke down while three women were in labor and about to give birth. Since state law required that newborns be weighed, the hospital was in a jam. The only scale in town was out at the lake in a bait shop, so the hospital administrator sent an orderly to borrow it. He returned in time and all three babies were born and properly weighed. The average weight of those new little Texans was 18 and a half pounds, a new state record.

A Difficult Choice The fisherman was getting on in years and went in to see the doctor for a physical. After checking him over, the doctor advised that he take life slower, do more fishing, and give up half his sex life. "Ok, doc," replied the Texan, "but which half shall I give up, thinking about it or talking about it?

Close Call The Texan went up north on vacation and naturally had to do some fishing. He was sitting on the bank when a stranger walked up and asked how he was doing.

"Not too good today, but I took forty trout out of here yesterday," ol' Tex replied.

"Do you know who I am?" asked the stranger.

"Don't have a clue," Tex replied.

"Well, I'm the local game warden and there is a ten-trout limit."

"And do you know who I am?" asked the Texan.

"Not yet," the warden replied.

The Texan laid down his pole and stood up. "Well, sir," he said, "let me introduce myself. I'm the biggest gawd damned liar the state of Texas ever produced."

Sign from the original Goode Company Barbecue restaurant in Houston: Old fishermen never die, they just can't raise their rods.

That old philosopher Az Tex once observed: The most boring thing in the world would be to go away on a week long fishing trip with a game warden.

Sad but True Why is it that the only days the fish are ever biting are yesterday and tomorrow.

A Texas Axiom The biggest fish always get away.

Corollary: Nothing makes a fish grow faster than almost being caught.

He May not be Kidding My friend James Schulenberger, from down Brenham way, swears the fishing is so good in that part of the state that you have to hide behind a tree to bait your hook. Otherwise, the fish just jump out of the water and take the bait right out of your hand and nothin' is harder to do than catch a fish bare-handed.

Sign seen in a bait shop in East Texas:

> Early to bed,
> early to rise.
> Fish all day,
> make up lies.

That old philosopher Az Tex believes that fishing is the hardest way on earth to take it easy.

Truth in Advertising The following want ad appeared in the personals of the *Fort Worth Star Telegram:* Wanted, attractive female who owns a boat and likes to fish. Should be a good cook and housekeeper. Must be willing to clean fish and dig worms for bait. Send photo of boat and motor.

Oldest of All Texas Fishing Jokes The Texan was up north visiting some relatives and naturally the conversation just sort of drifted around to fishing. Everyone took turns telling his story about the biggest fish he ever caught. Finally, someone asked the Texan, "Say, what is the biggest fish you ever caught down in Texas?"

The Texan thought for a minute, as if trying to remember, and finally said, "I expect the biggest fish I ever caught was a wide-mouth Texas black bass."

"How big was he?" someone asked.

"Wasn't a he, it was a she." the Texan replied. "And she measured a little over twelve inches."

"Twelve inches, that's not very big at all," someone commented.

"But gentlemen," the Texan said, "you must remember, down in Texas we measure 'em by the distance between their eyes."

Second Oldest of All Fishing Jokes A Texan had been entertaining some northern friends for hours with his tales of fishing in Texas. At every opportunity, the guests would try to outfox the grizzled old Texan and at every turn, the Texan was worthy of the challenge.

Finally after talking freshwater fish for a while, the Texan turned to saltwater fishing out in the Gulf of Mexico. "We were fishing for . . ." the Texan started but someone interrupted by suggesting "Terrapin."

The Texan shook his head. Quickly another guest suggested "Great white shark," but again the Texan shook his head. The third guest said sarcastically, "I suppose you were fishing for whales."

The old Texan smiled. "No, sir," he said, "we were using whales for bait."

A Texas Axiom The two happiest days in a man's life are the day he buys a boat and the day he sells it.

You would think that in Texas, a state known for tall tales and big liars, it would be impossible to find the biggest single lie. Not true. I met a man the other day who claimed he once met an honest fisherman. If that's not the biggest lie in Texas, I don't know what is.

What's Your Reason? There are generally two reasons a man goes fishing. He either wants to catch fish or he's not allowed to drink at home.

Then there was the Texas marriage counselor who wondered how many marriages might be saved if the husband would have as much patience with his wife as he does with fish.

Texas Riddle No. 14: Do you know the difference between a golfer and a fisherman? See answer page.

Two Texas lawyers, who were partners in their own firm, took the day off and went fishing. They were sitting out in the middle of a lake drowning some worms when one had a horrible thought. "I think," he said, "that I left the office safe open when we left."

"Never mind," said the other, "we're both here."

Figures Don't Lie An accountant, who was also an avid fisherman, was forced to give up the sport. He ran a cost analysis and found that all the fish he caught last year cost an average of $82.55 per pound.

Sign seen on a church marquee one Saturday afternoon: Fishing forecast for tomorrow, poor. We expect to see everyone in church.

Good Question The little Texan listened carefully as the Sunday school teacher explained all about Noah taking two of each species of animals aboard the ark and then keeping them there for forty days and forty nights. When she finished, the teacher asked for questions and the little Texan raised his hand. "Teacher, I was wondering. Did the ark have a live-well on it?"

"A live-well, what's that?" asked the teacher.

"A live-well is where you put fish to keep then alive after you've caught them."

"Well no, I don't think the ark had a live-well," the teacher concluded,

"Well then," the young Texan continued, "if ol' Noah took two of every kind of animal on board the ark, how do you suppose he kept the fish alive for forty days?"

Best Ever My nomination for best ever fishing joke is: The Texas fisherman called the doctor one morning in a real panic. "Doc," he exclaimed in an excited voice, "the baby has swallowed a fish hook."

"Ok, now don't panic," the doctor said. "Just get the baby to the hospital as soon as possible."

Five minutes later the doctor's phone rang again and it was the same fisherman. "Never mind, doc," he said in a calm voice, "I found another hook."

15

Signs of the Times

Texans Beware!

**We're Watching
the Wrong River**

Although Texans are most often known for their gift of gab, on occasion the Texas wit really shows through on signs, in the newspaper, on billboards, and sundry other written or printed sources. Perhaps the most famous of all Texas signs was once seen written in charcoal on a dug-out in a desolate part of West Texas. It simply stated: 20 miles to water, 10 miles to wood, 6 inches to hell. Gone back east to wife's family. Make yourself at home.

There have been plenty of other examples of Texas written wit. The proof follows.

Cafe Signs

Some of the most fertile grounds for Texas written humor are signs in eating establishments. Whether in an East Texas cafe, a South Texas BBQ joint, or any Texas truck stop, you are apt to see some written humor. Here's a generous sampling.

When you get to the end of your rope, tie a knot and hang on.

A Diet is nothing but Waist Management.

God please don't let me die while I'm on a diet.

I keep trying to lose weight but it finds me.

If we put too much meat on your sandwich, please complain.

If we don't please you, tell us, not others.

Don't criticize your husband's judgement.
Remember, he married you.

Keep this place in mind,
a better one is hard to find.

BBQ duck is always in season.

When you're in the dog house,
you are always welcome here.

Not responsible
for husbands or wives
strayed, lost, or stolen

Gentlemen will behave, others must.

Illiterate? Sign up here for free help.

ETC. Something you use to make people
think you know more than you do

Doing good is no fun unless you're caught in the act.

This country would be better off if we
had more whittlers and less chiselers.

Prompt service, no matter how long it takes.

Waitress wanted, experience necessary but not required.

I buy my food F.O.B.
Pay for it C.O.D.
Serve it P.D.Q.
How can I live on I.O.U?

Courteous and efficient self-service.

Curb service inside

Our food is like mother used to cook before she took up bridge.

What foods these morsels be.

My nomination for second runner up in the Texas cafe sign competition was seen in the original Goode Company Barbecue in Houston, Texas:

VYISDER
ZOMENYMOR
ORZIZAZZIZ
DANDER
IZ ORZIZ

If you absolutely, positively cannot figure it out, see Riddle Answer No. 15 on the answer page.

My nomination for first runner up in the Texas cafe sign competition was seen in a West Texas greasy spoon cafe: We only serve sausage made from pigs that died happy.

Finally, my nomination for best ever Texas cafe sign was once seen hanging in a Fort Worth establishment: As a hog roots for his food, he throws his weight on the right hind leg. All our hams come from the left side — they're the tenderest."

Money Matters

The question of how patrons pay their bill has often been the object of Texas sign humor. The oldest such sign was, of course, the all-time favorite: In God we trust, the rest pay cash. There have been more:

Second Oldest of All Texas Cafe Signs We have a deal with the bank. They don't serve chicken-fried steaks and we don't cash checks.

In a Fort Worth Company We cash checks only for men above eighty years of age — when accompanied by both parents.

From a Hamburger Joint in Plano We'd love to cash your check. Unfortunately, we still have several from last year we're trying to collect on.

From a Houston Texaco Station Yes, we cash checks. There is a $20.00 limit and you must have 6 pieces of identification and leave $50.00 cash deposit until it clears.

A Forth Worth furniture store has a creative payment plan: Use our easy payment plan: 100% down, owe nothing.

In a West Texas Cafe Your credit is good with us, as long as it comes from Visa or Master Card.

In an Old-time Cafe We'll sympathize with you if your wife doesn't understand you; we'll hold your horse; we'll tend to your baby — but don't ask us to cash your check.

The Current Check Cashing Policy of a West Texas Store

1. You must have a current Texas drivers license
2. You must have two other forms of identification
3. You must have a day and evening phone number
4. Checks taken on local banks only
5. Check cashing fee in $ .65 (sixty five cents)
6. Personal check limit is $ .50 (fifty cents)

My personal favorite money matters sign was seen in San Antonio: We recognize all credit cards. We only *take* cash.

The Texas Bumper Sticker Hall of Fame

In addition to the members of the Texas Bumper Sticker Hall of Fame already cited, here are some other candidates.

A Bumper Sticker that was bound to happen. You have doubtless seen numerous bumper stickers using a heart to indicate people "love" things such as cats, dogs, horses, certain cars, and the like. This one answer to all those bumper stickers was recently seen in Plano, Texas.

Seen in Austin:

No man's life, liberty, or prosperity is
safe when the legislature is in session.

Seen in Austin : Avoid cliches like the plague

Good teachers cost more
Bad teachers cost most

Seen in Dallas.

Seen in South Texas:

   If this car was a horse, they would have already shot it.

Seen in Dallas:

   Diets are for those who are thick and tired of it.

A favorite for those of us who were born in Fort Worth.

Seen in South Texas:

   Leave passing on the curves to beauty contest judges

From Around the State:

   Honk if you love Texas

   Yankee by birth,
   Texan by choice

One of the best all-time bumper stickers seen in Texas was popular a few years ago when Southwest Airlines decked out their stewardesses in skimpy hot pants. The bumper stickers simply read:

   Down With Hot Pants.

Billboards

Frequently, Texas humor shows up in large letters on billboards along the miles and miles and miles of Texas highways. Strangely enough, one of the most famous Texas billboards wasn't even in the Lone Star State. During World War II, the contribution made by the state of Texas was somewhat legendary. In fact there was some talk that if the other states didn't start helping, Texas was gonna pull out of the war and prolong it for ten years. To preclude that possibility, the state of California erected several large billboards urging Californians to "Buy Bonds and help Texas win the war."

Naturally, there have also been some interesting, entertaining, and even enlightening billboards inside the state of Texas. The following is but a small sample.

Back in the days before someone discovered the advisability of burying power lines underground instead of stringing them overhead, broken power lines were a danger to your health and well being. Over in Fort Worth, the A. F. South Electric Company once put up a huge billboard showing some broken lines menacing a house. The huge headline read: Let us check your shorts.

To promote its classified advertising section:

Cars go faster in the *Dallas Times Herald.*

Seen on a freeway in Fort Worth Texas:

New Braunfels may have the best wurst
but Dallas has the best newspaper.
Times Herald

To promote its basketball reporting, the *Dallas Morning News* commissioned a billboard showing a basketball coming through a paper beside the headline: Fast Breaking Coverage.

Padre Island claims on a current billboard:

Best beach, 365 rays a year.

On I35 going from Dallas toward Oklahoma, Stuckey's once had a giant billboard asking motorists to:

Eat with us
Get gas.

A South Texas exterminator advertised:

Just say no to bugs

Seen on Stemmons Freeway in Dallas:

Honk if you love Elvis,
turn right if you love Chili's.

Suites are getting popular in Texas and they are finding their way onto the billboards. One hotel advertises A Suite Deal. Another offers A great Suite for a sweet deal.

If you stay in a certain Corsicana motel you will: Spend a night not a fortune.

The "Super pile up ahead" mentioned on I35 south of Dallas is actually an all-you-can-eat buffet at Pizza Inn.

Wonder Cave in San Marcos encourages you to "See an earthquake from the inside." On another billboard they give you the location of the earthquake: Deep in the heart of Texas.

From the Dallas Flower Mart comes a subtle hint:

Tulips today, two lips tonight.

From the American Cancer Society comes a not so subtle hint. A sunbather is depicted beside the headline: Working on a killer tan.

At the Taco Cabanna in Austin you can: Peso little, Eat so much.

With the popularity of flea markets everywhere in Texas and Sea World in San Antonio, it was bound to happen. In Austin there's a giant billboard advertising: Fleaworld.

Sounds Good A Texas plumber once used a billboard to advise prospective customers: Our Royal Flush Beats Your Full House.

A Forth Worth billboard once asked the question: Tired of walking on water? It was sponsored by Roto Rooter Plumbing.

Then there is the billboard urging Dallasites to: Come on in for a test ride. It's sponsored by Weir's furniture and is advertising rocking chairs.

Another subtle hint from the American Cancer Society: Share the cost of living.

And you Thought it was Troy Aikman   According to the billboard:

Dallas #1 Draft Choice is Miller.

One of the most famous Texas billboards of all time was courtesy of Stanley Marsh III up in the panhandle. Although details of the story often vary, Stanley was having some trouble with a local church. Seems they were interested in building a little too close to the Marsh property. After repeated attempts to reconcile the problem, Stanley gave up and erected a giant billboard proclaiming: Future Home of World's Largest Poisonous Snake Farm. His problems with the church were solved.

My nomination for best ever Texas billboard was recently put up on the infamous Central Expressway in Dallas. The sign was sponsored by Oak Farms Dairy and featured a large glass of milk beside the words: Fresh squeezed.

Town Signs

Occasionally some smaller towns in Texas come up with their own wit and wisdom on signs:

Sign in Hondo, Texas: Welcome. This is God's country, please don't drive through it like hell.

The best use of one sign may have been in Pyote, Texas. One side of the sign read: You are now entering Pyote. The other side of the sign read: You are now leaving Pyote.

Outside Amarillo, Texas, someone once put up a small hand-made sign:

The last one out, cut off the lights.

As you enter a small town in South Texas you see the sign:

"Drive slow and see our town; drive fast and see our jail."

Then there is the best ever Texas town sign:

Everybody is somebody in Luckenbach.

During 1936, the main Texas Centennial celebration was held in Dallas, a fact that didn't sit too well with the Fort Worth city fathers, especially Amon Carter. To fight back, Fort Worth decided to host their own Frontier Celebration and they hired the then famous entertainer Billy Rose to run the affair. One of the first things Rose did was commission a giant sign to be erected on a building opposite the entrance to the Dallas fair grounds proclaiming: Go to Dallas for culture, Come to Fort Worth for Whoopee. Because the sign was totally legal, the Dallas city fathers had to condemn the building to get it removed.

Seen in New Braunfels, Texas. Apparently someone has solved the problem of a shortage of hospital beds in small towns.

The most famous Texas town sign of all time once spanned the main street of Greenville, Texas proclaiming: The blackest land and whitest people. When it was finally decided the sign was in poor taste, it was changed to: The blackest land and the nicest people. Eventually even that didn't work and the sign was removed.

Where's Johnny?

Where to Go   Occasionally, visitors to Texas are a bit perplexed when they have to visit a public necessary room. Some business establishments in Texas have gotten creative when designating which rest room is which. Here's my personal collection of rest room signs seen in the Lone Star State:

Buckeroos — Buckerooettes
Wranglers — Wranglerettes
Bull Riders — Barrel Racers
The Bull Pen — The Hen House
Roosters — Hens
Stallions — Mares
Bread Winners — Bread Spenders
Aggies — Maggies
Bulls — Heifers
Astronauts — Astronets
Cowboys — Cowgirls
Good ol' Boys — Little Darlin's

My all-time favorite, and quite possibly the best ever, was found in a little cafe in East Texas that specialized in fried chicken. The rest rooms were appropriately labeled:

Crowers — Setters

Of course, once you get into the men's room, the signs often continue. The most popular and most often seen is: We aim to please, you aim too, please. But there are more:

Don't throw cigarette butts into the urinal,
they get soggy and are hard to light.

Ball players with short bats stand close to the plate.
Stand close, don't flatter yourself.

Soldiers with short rifles, stay within firing range.

Smile. You're on closed circuit television.

Keep your butt out!
This is not an ash tray.

What's in a Name?

Occasionally, Texas entrepreneurs will get very creative in their choice of business names. The following are some examples:

Software retailer in Dallas: Soft Warehouse
Beauty shop down on the Gulf Coast: Curl Harbor
Restaurant: Souper Salad
Beauty shop in Amarillo: Curl up and Dye
Restaurant: The Feed Bag
Mobile home dealer near Dallas: Sherlock Mobile Homes
Trailer rental: Wee Haul
Smoke shop: Tobacco Lane
Warehouse in central Texas: The Best Little Warehouse in Texas
A Texas beauty salon: The Best Little Hairhouse in Texas
Another beauty salon: Debbie does Hair
Used clothing dealer in Houston: Wear it again, Sam
Another hair care shop: Hair Force One
Shoe store: Bunions and Bows
Antique shop: Simply Ewe Antiques
Child care center: Wee Care

The Best May be Yet to Come Lu Smith, an old friend, has been saying for years she's going to open a bar and call it Carls Bad Tavern.

A Mixed Herd of Miscellaneous Written Wit

What follows is a collection of wit that has shown up in the newspaper, on some sign somewhere, on a bumper sticker, or almost anywhere else in Texas.

Double Meaning? Capital Bank, which uses the Pulse ATM's, hung out a banner inviting customer to: "Check our Pulse." Considering the state of banking in Texas, that could have been a dangerous sign.

Motto of the Highland Park Pharmacy. We have it, we will get it, or it isn't made.

Sign in the office of Red Adair, world famous oil well fire fighter: I said maybe and that's final.

From the Texas T-Shirt Hall of Fame.

Headline from the San Antonio Express: Louis Wins and Loses Union Suit

Sign seen on the side of a wrecker:

24 HOUR SERVICE
WE'RE ALWAYS
ON OUR TOWS

Sign in a West Texas diet center: We make alterations to your birthday suit.

King Fisher was one of the true Texas characters of the old west. Before he and Marshal Ben Thompson were gunned down in a San Antonio theater, Fisher lived on a South Texas ranch. And he liked to be left alone, so much so that he erected a sign on the road running through his property that proclaimed:

This is King Fisher's Road
Take Another One

The friends of the Amarillo Library have various sayings they use on buttons, T-shirts, and the like. Here's a sampling:

I'm a Happy Booker
Ignorance Is Not Bliss
Bookworms Do It Between the Covers
Novel Lover
Libraries Are User Friendly
I Read Banned Books
Hooked On Books
I Read Texan

Headline from Wichita Falls: Enraged Cow Injures Farmer With Ax.

Sign on Central Expressway in Dallas that seems to indicate someone has come up with a new invention that might have promise:

BRASS BEDS
FAX

Sign seen on a desk at NASA Headquarters in Houston:

OUT TO LAUNCH

One of the best signs in Texas if you are driving north out of San Antonio. For years Selma, Texas has been known as a premier speed trap. Forewarned is forearmed.

According to an El Paso paper: A Mr. Blank lost a finger when a poisoned dog to which he was administering an anecdote bit him.

Headline from El Paso: Bride gets replaced on Highway 82.

Preserve Texas water, Drink Texas wine.

From the Texas Bumper Sticker Hall of Fame. Seen on a car in Lubbock, Texas.

Sign in a San Antonio Hotel:

SEE US FOR A SUCCESSFUL AFFAIR

How's That Again? One Texas paper reported: According to the complaint, Mrs. Blank says her husband started amusing her three days before their wedding.

Sign, handwritten, supposedly hung over a door at Carswell Air Force Base in Fort Worth: Do not start vast projects with half vast ideas.

Your Pullin' My Leg A good friend swears he saw this sign on an Amarillo construction site: NO UNAUTHORIZED TREASPASSING.

Sign, handmade, in a Dallas hospital: Thank you for not Croaking.

How's That Again? Someone once stuck a handwritten sign on the door of an optometrist's office: If you can't read this, come on in. Underneath someone scribbled: Eyes examined while you wait.

News Item From the *Andrews County News*: Refreshments of cake squares, iced in pink and glue, were served.

Headline from down in the state capital:

Jury Gets Drunk
Driving Case Here

All-time best Christmas greeting: "Twas the night before Christmas and all through the house not a creature was stirring, not even a mouse." XYZ Exterminating

Confusing Sign Kathy Ward was a nice little Yankee girl who had the sense to marry a Texas boy. After moving to Texas, Kathy accompanied her husband and father-in-law on a deer hunting trip. As they bounced along in the pickup near Stephenville, Texas, Kathy suddenly asked, "Are we near the ocean?"

Her husband said no and wanted to know why she asked. "Well," explained Kathy, "I saw a sign back there offering 200 Acres, Coastal." When her husband stopped laughing, he explained that coastal meant the type of grass, not the location.

Classified Ad in the Lubbock *Avalanche Journal:* Need a sympathetic companion? Basset puppies are all ears.

El Paso, Texas is known for having sunshine almost every day of the year. Once after a particularly long spell of bad weather finally broke, the *El Paso Herald Post* reported with a large headline: PRODIGAL SUN RETURNS.

Apparently, during some road construction between Dallas and Waco, the contractor felt obliged to remind equipment operators that power lines are up.

Headline from *North Fort Worth* newspaper: Local Man has Longest Horns in All Texas.

T-Shirt seen in Dallas and a lot of other places in Texas:

> We Drill 'em Deeper
> Ewing Oil, Inc.

The *Dallas Times Herald* once used the following headline over a story about a church organ that had been stolen: ORGAN TRANSPLANTED

Truth in Advertising The following want ad appeared in the *San Antonio Evening News:* Executive Director, from 24 to 40. To sit at desk from 9 to 5 and watch other people work. Must be willing to play golf every other afternoon. Salary, over $350 to start. WE DON'T HAVE THIS JOB! WE JUST THOUGHT WE'D LIKE TO SEE IN PRINT WHAT EVERYONE IS APPLYING FOR.

Double Billings on Movie marquees:

Houston: LADY GODIVA — RUN FOR COVER

Fort Worth: AN AMERICAN IN PARIS — THE BIG HANGOVER

Sign on a pleasure ship in the Gulf of Mexico: Don't spit, remember the Galveston flood.

A Sign in an old-time dentist office: The yanks are coming.

Headline from Houston: San Leon Man Quits Raising Hogs for Fruit

Sign on a little store in Fort Worth: Customers wanted — no experience necessary.

An example of some sad signs that have been seen all too frequently in Texas during recent years.

Headline from a Dallas paper: Thugs Eat, Then Rob Proprietor

Sign at a roadside fruit stand: Our watermelons have a heart.

Headline from Galveston: Dog in Bed, asks Divorce.

Sign in an Olney Hotel: Hot and Cold water, hot in summer, cold in winter; all modern conveniences; rates after I look 'em over.

A personal favorite sign was seen near the Fort Worth City Hall. Apparently, the Fort Worth City fathers thought they could improve on the popular signs asking people to buckle up their seat belts. In Cowtown, the signs read, above an illustration of the seat belt being fastened:

> Hook 'em Up, Ya'll.

What About the Seen Ones? From a Midland paper: Through blinding fog and raging storm, alert salesmen guard against unseen perils.

Sign in an antique store: There's no present like the past.

Sign in a Fort Worth shop: Satisfaction guaranteed. All sales final.

I'd Like to See it Done From the *Fort Worth Star Telegram:* All during the testimony he hardly moved in his chair. For the most of the time he rested his head on his chin.

Sign in an antique store: Don't pass me — buy

Best Ever Perhaps the best ever advertising sign was seen recently in rural Texas on the side of a septic tank company truck: No one sticks his nose in our business.

Sign seen in a San Antonio gun shop:

> No matter how good your aim is in life,
> you won't amount to hardly nothing
> if you don't squeeze the trigger.

Sign seen near Muleshoe, Texas. Apparently the junk dealer was both religious and short on sign material. Outside his establishment, a single handmade sign proclaimed:

> Jesus
> Inside
> Used
> Refrigerators

But Did They Catch Anything? From the *Waco News-Tribune:* The district game warden filed four complaints, charging illegal fishing in Judge J. J. Padgett's court.

Sign on well rig: Well drilling, the only business where you start at the top

Sign in a Dallas boutique:

> Shoplifters will be beaten,
> whipped, drug behind a
> horse, shot, and hung.
> Survivors will be prosecuted.

Announcement from the Corsicana newspaper: The Psychology Club will meet in regular session on Wednesday afternoon at three o'clock. The subject for discussion will be "The Use and Application of Powder."

Goss on Ross, a used car dealer in Dallas has been selling cars for more years than many people can remember. Here's the sign that explains his prices:

> New cars: $89.50 down
> Used cars: $79.50 down
> Get to work cars: $69.50 down
> Get to work late cars: $59.50 down
> Work cars for temporary jobs: $49.50 down

Sign at an auction company: We put U in the action

Could You Make One Like Linda Carter? The following advertisement appeared in an El Paso paper: Widows made to order. Send us your specifications.

Sign over the sink at Wordware Publishing, Inc. in Plano: Your Mother Doesn't Work Here so Please Clean Up After Yourself.

Road sign in Houston: Go with the flow, take it slow.

Sign in Central Texas near Austin proclaims: "We top the best." It's sponsored by Texas Hatters.

Sign in a fabric shop in West Texas: Virgin wool comes from sheep that can run fast.

Slogan of Spoetzl Brewery, makers of Shiner Beer: Let the beer do the talking!

Actual advertisement from the Pittsburgh, Texas newspaper:

BUFFALO CAFE
for
GOOD THINGS TO EAT *and* DRINK
FISH MARKET
People's Funeral Home
for
NICE JOBS and GOOD COACH
Service with a smile.

Sign inside the office of a noted Texas high school coach's office: Winning isn't Everything, but it sure beats the hell out of the alternative.

T-Shirt seen on a young man at Dallas Love Field airport.
On the front it read: **Q:** Why Texas?
On the back it read: **A:** Because I placed out of A&M.

Another double sided T-Shirt from the University of Texas.
On the front it read: **U B U**
On the back it read: **I Be a**

Sign at an East Texas auto repair shop:

We do precision guesswork.

Classified Ad from West Texas: Wanted clean, nice girl for general spousework.

Sign on a pawn shop in Irving:

Please remove ski mask and
unload gun before entering.

Classified Ad in Dallas: What have you got to offer in exchange for beautiful wire-haired female?

Sign in the offices of Dallas Motors:

This property
protected by
PIT BULL
with AIDS

Sign seen in many offices of Yankees who have relocated to Texas.

Good Advice From a Houston Texas paper comes the following warning: For cockroaches, don't use sodium fluoride because children or cherished pets may eat the sodium fluoride instead of the cockroaches.

T-Shirt in the offices of KFMX in Lubbock: "I survived the Lubbock Traffic Circle." Big Ed Wilks advises the infamous Lubbock traffic circle is no more. It has been replaced by a traffic square.

Sign on fence in a Houston suburb:

> Warning!
> Premises protected
> by Smith and Wesson.

Sign on another fence, in Garland:

> Warning!
> Mean Dog,
> Meaner owner.

Signs of the Times In its efforts to drum up recruits, the Texas Army National Guard has recently been displaying special advertising messages at movie theaters around the state:

> Beat around the bush with us!

> Let's tank it up this weekend.

> If you're into heavy metal,
> spend a weekend with us.

Perhaps the saddest sign ever seen in Texas:

NCNB

And then there was the headline in a recent edition of the *Dallas Times Herald:* Need a brain? Firm caters to mail orders.

And finally, a real favorite among Texans. The following poem, by author unknown, was framed and hung up in the original Goode Company Barbecue restaurant in Houston Texas:

The Cowboy At Rest
When my old soul hunts range and rest,
beyond the last divide;
Just plant me in some stretch of west
that's sunny, lone, and wide.
Let cattle rub my tombstone down
and coyotes mourn their kin.
Let horses paw and tromp the moun
but don't you fence it in.

16

Parting Shots

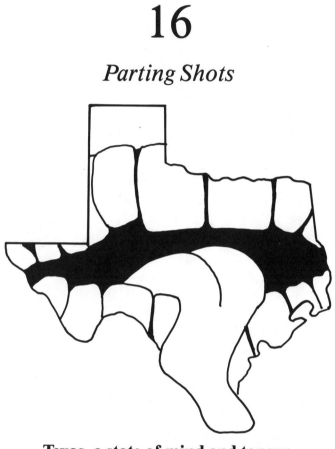

Texas, a state of mind and tongue
Billy Porterfield
Austin American Statesman

Texans have always been known as talkers. While a lot of what has come out of the mouths of Texans would be labeled as "braggadocios," some good ol' boys and little darlin's from the Lone Star State have, on occasion, managed to speak with wisdom and insight. Since this book is finished, I'll leave you with some Texas thoughts to ponder:

A popular saying is that Texas is a state of mind. In a recent column reviewing the book *This Dog'll Hunt,* Billy Porterfield of the *Austin American Statesman* expanded that saying to: "Texas is a State of Mind and Tongue."

One of the most loved and respected Texans of all time, Hugh Roy Cullen, once said, "Don't give anyone reason to feel insulted, and don't ever take an insult."

Henri Castro, early Texas colonist, offered this advice for a happy life: "Begin your day with labor and end it with laughter."

Texas Ranger manager Bobby Valentine said, "You're only as good as the information you get."

Who can forget Davy Crockett's immortal words, "I leave this rule for others when I am dead: Be always sure you're right, then go ahead."

Hondo Crouch, the classic all-time Texas character said, "Make good or make room."

Texan Trammel Crow, the nation's landlord, once said, "There's as much risk in doing nothing as in doing something." It was also Mr. Crow who said, "Work is more fun than fun."

J. Frank Dobie, perhaps the all-time favorite Texas writer, once offered some off-handed advice: "Conform and be dull."

Another J. Frank Dobie observation, "Thought employs ideas, but having an idea is not the same thing as thinking. A rooster in a pen of hens has an idea."

Trammel Crow's thought on ideas: "In business, the idea is the thing. Don't make it any more complicated than that. If your ideas are worthy, you will succeed."

A favorite saying of Billie Sol Estes, "You win by losing, hold on by letting go, increase by diminishing and multiply by dividing."

James Ferguson, the only governor Texas has ever impeached to date, once urged, "Never say die, say damn."

One of the most famous Texas quotes came from old-time Texas Ranger Captain Bill McDonald. He said "No man that's in the wrong can stand up against a fellow that's in the right and keeps a coming." That old philosopher Az Tex, who has helped us through this book, would add a postscript to that quote: "No man can stand up against a female, whether she's in the right or the wrong."

As proof that old Az Tex may be absolutely correct, consider the immortal words of Farrah Fawcett, one of the best lookin' women to ever come out of Texas. She said, "God made men stronger but not necessarily more intelligent. He gave women intuition and femininity. And used properly, that combination easily jumbles the brain of any man I've ever met."

America's most decorated war hero, Texan Audie Murphy, once observed, "In life, quality is what counts, not quantity."

Dutch Meyer, legendary coach at TCU, was once asked how he felt about being a good loser. He replied, "You can be a good loser, but you should always bleed a little."

Mr. Sam Rayburn offered this advice for making progress, "If you want to get along, go along."

It was also Mr. Sam who said, "The size of a man has nothing to do with his height."

And Again From Mr. Sam "The greatest ambition a man can have is to be a just man."

And Finally From Mr. Sam "Having good common sense isn't enough — you have to exercise it." That quote probably explains the old Texas saying: "Having a lot of horse sense doesn't keep a man from acting like a jackass."

Charles Tandy, founder of, you guessed it, Tandy Corporation, once observed, "To catch a mouse you've got to make noise like a cheese."

A Sam Houston rule that everyone should probably follow: "My rule is, when my hand is in the lion's mouth not to strike him on the nose."

Hugh Roy Cullen, who once almost drowned in a whirlpool, observed: "Anybody can swim into a whirlpool. It's coming out of it that counts."

Another Hondo Crouch observation, "The world's greatest thing is to be simple, but it is so hard to be simple."

Here's some advice from Texan John Wesley Hardin, considered by many to be the deadliest gunfighter ever to strap on a Colt: "If you wish to be successful in life, be temperate and control your passions; if you don't, ruin and death is the inevitable result."

A pointed observation from Lyndon Johnson: "We don't all see everything alike. If we did, we would all want the same wife."

According to Sam Houston, "Dead ducks need no killing."

In Texas a popular saying is: "Don't change horses in midstream." Az Tex advises it is also desirable not to change diapers in midstream.

Texan Liz Carpenter, explaining her fear of flying: "In my heart, I know the Wright brothers were wrong."

Mary Kay Ash, founder of the world famous Mary Kay Cosmetics firm, believes men and women should receive equal pay for equal work. To substantiate her position she said, "I can't believe that God intended for a woman's brain to be worth 50 cents on the dollar."

Jim Bob Boyd of KILT radio in Houston once offered this piece of advice, "When driving, you are not invisible so don't pick your nose."

Audie Murphy, perhaps the bravest Texan of all time once explained, "Bravery is just determination to do a job that you know has to be done."

Former Texas Governor, Secretary of the Navy, and Presidential candidate John Connally once said, "In short, if you are not willing to be quoted by name, you should not be speaking."

Want To Live a Long Life? You might follow the advice of Sam Rayburn: "My prescription would be to keep busy, do not get angered about little things, eat plenty, sleep long, and never feel like you are getting old."

And who can forget the immortal words of two-time Texas Governor Bill Clements: "Nothing is ever so bad that it can't be worse. Or better."

And finally, my own humble contribution: "Until we meet again, keep your wagon between the ditches and the lightnin' bugs out of the buttermilk."

Answers

A Day That Will Live in Infamy Without question, the darkest day in the history of Texas was January 3, 1959. That's the day Alaska was admitted to the Union making Texas the second largest state.

Riddle No. 1: What has a mouth but never speaks, and a bed but never sleeps? The Brazos River

Riddle No. 2: Do you know the difference between a bird and a Texas oilman? The bird can still put down a deposit on a new Cadillac.

Riddle No. 3: Do you know the difference between the Titantic and the Texas oil business? The Titantic had a band.

Riddle No. 4: What do Dolly Parton, Morgana the kissing bandit, and a Texas oilman have in common? They all know what big busts are like.

Riddle No. 5: Do you know how to become a Texas oil millionaire these days? Start out as a Texas oil billionaire.

Riddle No. 6: Do you know the difference between a Texas bird dog and a Texas politician? A Texas bird dog is a pointer and a setter; a Texas politician is a disappointer and an upsetter.

Riddle No. 7: What has four legs, eats hay, sleeps in a stable, and can see equally well from either end? A blind horse.

Riddle No. 8: What do a woman and a cow patty have in common? The older they get, the easier they are to pick up.

Riddle No. 9: Why did the chicken go only halfway across the road? She wanted to lay it on the line.

Riddle No. 10: Do you know how many Aggies it takes to milk a cow? Five, one to hold a teat and four to shake the cow.

Riddle No. 11: What do you call a smart person on the A&M campus? A visitor.

Riddle No. 12: Do you know how to tell when an Aggie has been working on a computer? By all the white-out on the screen.

Postscript Riddle What do the Aggies call a parachutist whose chute doesn't open? A Super Collider.

Riddle No. 13: How do you drive an Aggie crazy? Put him in a round room and ask him to stand in the corner.

Riddle No. 14: Do you know the difference between a golfer and a fisherman? A golfer doesn't have to have any fish to prove his score.

Riddle No. 15:

VYISDER — why is there
ZOMENYMOR — so many more
ORZIZAZZIZ — horses asses
DANDER — than there
IZ ORZIZ — is horses

This Dog'll Hunt

The ultimate Texas dictionary! *This Dog'll Hunt* contains thousands of the popular Texas sayings so common in the language of the state. All entries are arranged in the familiar dictionary format so the material is easy to use. As a bonus, many interesting quotations and stories are included to make this a dictionary that everyone will want to read and find difficult to put down.

This Dog'll Hunt includes an introduction by Texas State Treasurer Ann Richards, the lady who charmed a nation at the 1988 Democratic National Convention. In addition, each letter of the alphabet is introduced with a cartoon featuring "Adobe," a lovable rascal of a Texas hound dog.

This book is destined to be a classic. It is an absolute must for anyone who wants to talk like a Texan or to simply understand what a Texan is saying. *This Dog'll Hunt* is the perfect choice for anyone searching for that unique gift for a friend or relative "up North."

1-55622-125-8 • **$12.95**
softbound • 277 pages • 6 x 9
1-55622-126-6 • **$14.95**
hardbound • 277 pages • 6 x 9

Rainy Days in Texas Workbook

This book is a new entertainment package that is perfect for occupying kids on those rainy days when they can't go outside to play. All the material is presented to subtly teach youngsters something about Texas history while they are entertaining themselves.

Rainy Days in Texas Workbook contains a wonderland of easy-to-do projects including word search puzzles, do-it-yourself jigsaw puzzles and mobiles, some emergency coloring book pages, a Texas flag construction kit, connect-the-dots pictures and so much more. All the activities include easy-to-follow instructions that will increase the enjoyment of children while holding parental stress to an absolute minimum. Mothers and fathers will love the *Rainy Days in Texas Workbook* because it's like having a baby-sitter in a book. Grandparents will love the book because it makes a wonderful educational gift.

1-55622-130-4 • **$9.95**
softbound • 120 pages • 8 1/2 x 11

**Classic Clint: The Laughs and Times
of Clint Murchison, Jr.**
by Dick Hitt
>278 pages • 6 x 9
>softbound • 1-55622-146-0 • $14.95

Exploring the Alamo Legends
by Wallace O. Chariton
>288 pages • 6 x 9
>hardbound • 1-55622-132-0 • $18.95

Forget the Alamo
by Wallace O. Chariton
>344 pages • 6 x 9
>hardbound • 1-55622-134-7 • $18.95

The Great Texas Airship Mystery
by Wallace O. Chariton
>272 pages • 6 x 9
>hardbound • 1-55622-140-1 • $16.95

Kingmakers
byJohn R. Knaggs
>300 pages • 6 x 9
>softbound • 1-55622-245-9 • $12.95

100 Days in Texas: The Alamo Letters
by Wallace O. Chariton
>408 pages • 6 x 9
>softbound • 1-55622-131-2 • $14.95

Rainy Days in Texas Funbook
by Wallace O. Chariton
>160 pages • 6 x 9
>softbound • 1-55622-130-4 • $9.95

San Antonio Uncovered
by Mark Louis Rybczyk
>304 pages • 6 x 9
>softbound • 1-55622-145-0 • $12.95

Texas: An Owner's Manual
by Wallace O. Chariton
180 pages • 6 x 9
softbound • 1-55622-247-5 • $12.95

Texas Highway Humor
by Wallace O. Chariton
144 pages • 5½ x 8½
softbound • 1-55622-176-2 • $10.95

Texas Tales Your Teacher Never Told You
by Charles F. Eckhardt
224 pages • 6 x 9
softbound • 1-55622-141-X • $12.95

Texas Wit and Wisdom
by Wallace O. Chariton
252 pages • 5½ x 8½
softbound • 1-55622-135-5 • $9.95

That Cat Won't Flush
by Wallace O. Chariton
288 pages • 5½ x 8½
softbound • 1-55622-175-4 • $12.95

They Don't Have to Die
by Jim Dunlap
280 pages • 6 x 9
softbound • 1-55622-193-2 • $12.95

This Dog'll Hunt
by Wallace O. Chariton
300 pages • 5½ x 8½
softbound • 1-55622-126-6 • $14.95

To the Tyrants Never Yield
A Texas Civil War Sampler
by Kevin R. Young
280 pages • 6 x 9
softbound • 1-55622-143-6 • $14.95

Unsolved Texas Mysteries
by Wallace O. Chariton
272 pages • 6 x 9
softbound • 1-55622-136-3 • $16.95